PETE MARAVICH

※

MAGICIAN OF THE HARDWOOD

PETE MARAVICH

MAGICIAN OF THE HARDWOOD

MIKE TOWLE

Cumberland House
Nashville, Tennessee

Published by
Cumberland House Publishing, Inc.
431 Harding Industrial Drive
Nashville, TN 37211-3160

Cover design: Gore Studio, Inc.
Text design: John Mitchell

Library of Congress Cataloging-in-Publication Data

Towle, Mike.
    Pete Maravich : magician of the hardwood / [compiled by] Mike Towle.
        p. cm.
    Includes bibliographical references and index.
    ISBN 1-58182-374-6 (pbk. : alk. paper)
    1. Maravich, Pete, 1948—Anecdotes. 2. Maravich, Pete, 1948—Friends and associates. 3. Basketball players—United States--Biography. I. Title: Pete Maravich. II. Title.
GV884.M3 T69 2000
796.323'092—dc21
[B]
                                                                    00-064420

Printed in the United States of America
1 2 3 4 5 6 7—08 07 06 05 04 03

※※※

To the Pistol

※※※

CONTENTS

PREFACE

Every time I think about Pete Maravich, I think about Arkansas. That might sound strange for someone who grew up in Vermont (me) writing about a guy whose basketball career is most closely associated with Louisiana (Pistol Pete). But it's true, and I'm happy to explain.

I met Maravich in late December 1987 on a Delta flight from Little Rock to Dallas. The night before we had been at the Alabama-Arkansas nonconference basketball game (the Hogs belonged to the Southwest Conference in those days), Pete as a color commentator for USA Network and me as a college hoops writer for the *Fort Worth Star-Telegram*. During the return flight, I went back to Pete's seat and introduced myself. We chatted briefly and exchanged business cards, and that was that. Christmas came and went, and in early January I was back in Arkansas, this time holed up in a Fayetteville hotel because I was in town covering another Arkansas game. It was there that I was watching television when an announcement was made of Maravich's death that morning.

Maravich had died of a heart attack while playing a pickup basketball game in California. He was forty years old.

When I think of Maravich, I also think back to growing up in northern Vermont in the dead of winter, frequently shoveling snow off a neighbor's driveway and begging Mrs. Clark to turn on their porch light so I could shoot baskets until bedtime. I would pretend I was Pete Maravich pouring in forty or fifty points a game, although my playing in mittens precluded me from trying to spin the ball on my fingers. In Vermont in 1969, ESPN and nightly highlights of the Pistol were light-years away. All I had to go on in emulating Maravich were a few pictures of Pete in sports magazines and clippings that detailed the Pistol's latest scoring outbursts. It wasn't until years later that I discovered there was much more to Maravich than his just being a gunning-scoring machine: He was also a magician with the ball who could take it around, under, over, and between various body parts. He could also make incredible no-look passes on the run and even put in a few games of great defense when it was absolutely necessary, and his repertoire of shots bordered on infinity.

The easy way out when putting Maravich's life in perspective is describing him as a white Globetrotter who set scoring records in college because he played for his dad. On further inspection, Maravich is seen as a dedicated basketball savant and showman who might have been the consummate offensive player, a hoopster who could do it all, and did it all, on the court and off. He grew up with an alcoholic mother who would later commit suicide, and an abrasive yet accommodating pop who taught him the game, including most of the drills that made Pete so handy with a basketball in his hands. Pete, too, became a heavy drinker and also dabbled in activities with questionable spiritual influence, such as yoga and UFOs. But for about the last six years of his life, Maravich enthusiastically embraced Jesus Christ and Christianity, and he took his message of eternal peace and salvation to the masses as a compelling public speaker.

Maravich's life story has already been told in several books, most notably his autobiography, *Heir to a Dream*, which was published less than a year before his death. *Pete Maravich : Magician of the Hardwood* is neither autobiography nor biography, and readers here won't get a month-by-month, year-by-year rehash of his life and career. This is a compilation of candid and revealing memories of Maravich told, in their own words, by dozens of people who knew him well, whether as high school buddies, college teammates, his coaches, pro and college opponents, experts in the basketball media, or personal acquaintances from other sports.

Two of the main themes that come through in this book are, first, how Maravich's extraordinary style of basketball would hold up remarkably well today, twenty to thirty years later, as freshly innovative and contemporary; and, second, that his conversion to born-again Christianity was a genuine profession and was actually quite stunning, considering the reckless turns his life had taken before he was even thirty. Maravich was, and is, an inspiration for two entirely separate, sometimes conflicting, worlds.

Putting together a book like this is possible only with the cooperation of the many people who graciously consented to be interviewed. There was nothing in it for them, but they took time out from busy schedules to share remembrances, anecdotes, retrospective analyses, and testimonials of and about a man whose influence remains palpable a dozen years after his death. I won't list all the names of contributors here—read the book—but I thank you all for being forthcoming and insightful. As with any book of this nature, and I have done a few others in a similar mode, there was an element of "freeze-out"—the old four corners, if you will—when I attempted to contact people or acquaintances close to Maravich, but all in all it was a positive and fruitful experience.

Some of the people I contacted went above and beyond the call of duty in putting me in touch with others interviewed for this book. Bud Johnson, a crack PR flack who twice worked with Maravich, goes to the head of the class. Thanks, Bud, for sharing a part of yourself and for pointing me in the right directions. Mary LaStrapes, Donald Ray Kennard's legistlative assistant, was tireless in finding a way to work me into X-Ray's busy schedule on microscopic notice, and she then took it a step further by working her phone on my behalf when my schedule started to go awry. By the time I finished this book, Pat Fredericks in the LSU sports information office knew it was me as soon as she picked up the telephone. And not only did Pat dig through files to find valuable stuff about Maravich, she took time out from more important duties on her job description to do a ton of photocopying for me. Kent Lowe, LSU's basketball SID, was patient and helpful with my many queries.

Tim "Bone" Bourret, a great guy at Clemson and the embodiment of enthusiasm, as well as a trustworthy cohort during our days as student assistants in the Notre Dame sports information department, came through in crunch time. So did Jack McCallum of *Sports Illustrated*, Vanessa and Alexander Wolff, Paul Hetrick, Greg Bernbrock, Jeff Twist, Joann Thaxton, Jim Washington, Kim Turner, Arthur Triche, John Ferguson, Chuck Gallina, John Mengelt, Lesley Visser, Jim Barnett, Marty Blake, Raymond Ridder, Julie Fie, Jan Hubbard, John Black, Les Robinson, Brooks Downing, Robin Brendle, Tom Boerwinkle, Josh Krulewitz, and Ralph Jukkola. These and other people opened up their little black books and helped me with phone numbers, probably in turn betraying a few confidences along the way.

Ron Pitkin, John Mitchell, Ed Curtis, and the rest of the Cumberland House gang set a lot of picks for me, breaking me free for some easy lay-ups.

Pastor Maury Davis and the entire staff at Cornerstone Church in Nashville have ministered to me and my family in more ways than they can know. Ditto for Bob Nichols, Bill Kraftson, and Phil Scott.

While writing this book, I said good-bye for the last time to my ninety-seven-year-old grandfather, Roy Carpenter, the most selfless man I have ever met. He was heaven-sent. My parents, Bill and Anne Towle, have always been there for me, too. Ditto for my sisters, Kathy and Betsy.

My wife, Holley, and toddler son, Andrew, patiently watched as segments of family time slipped away while I hibernated for several weeks putting the finishing touches on this book. I love you, Holley and Andrew.

Finally, and I know Pistol Pete would echo me on this, I thank Jesus Christ for being my eternal advocate with God, our Father. Life still presents obstacles and anxieties, but having that safety net is an incredible source of confidence. I accepted Christ a little over a year after meeting Pete, and while he didn't proselytize to me, I believe he somehow planted a seed within me. By the way, his is the only business card I have never removed from my wallet.

PETE MARAVICH

MAGICIAN OF THE HARDWOOD

1

THE CAROLINA KID

Don't believe the myth. Pete Maravich was not born with a basketball in his hands. Truth is, that didn't happen until at least several hours later, courtesy of his dad, basketball-coaching junkie Peter "Press" Maravich. Maybe it was more than just a few hours later, at that. Pete Maravich himself said that he actually started playing basketball when he was seven years old, at which time his dad turned him into what young Pete called a basketball "android." From that point forward, Maravich was rarely without a basketball in his hands, to include lying in bed at night trying to go to sleep by practicing his shooting release with a basketball. Fingertip control . . . backspin on the shot . . . follow-through to the hoop. This was how he whittled away at the nocturnal anxiety, the ball bouncing to the floor when Pete finally lost consciousness performing his version of counting sheep.

Pete spent his life on the go. That was a characteristic ingrained in him by his gruff yet lovable dad, who followed his own dream of basketball coaching, starting out in

Pennsylvania and frequently pulling up roots while making career whistle stops in West Virginia, South Carolina, North Carolina, Louisiana, and, finally, back to North Carolina. Maravich wasn't settled while growing up. He and his family were moving every few years, forcing Pete to frequently make new friends and bust through cliques on his way to becoming a worldly young man turning college basketball on its ear while setting scoring records at LSU in his late teens and early twenties.

The one constant during Pete's many moves—and he had plenty more on the basketball court, where he was a dazzling ballhandling prodigy by the time he was in the sixth grade—was his basketball, and it helped him become acclimated to the many environments he bounced between up and down the Atlantic Coast and into the Deep South.

For the purpose of this oral history of Pete's life, sparing most of the details of the somewhat typically dysfunctional Maravich family dynamics, we pick up Pete in his youthful preteen days. School was just a clock-punching activity to be tolerated while he waited for classes to get out so he could either run out and find another game of pickup basketball or head over to his dad's college gymnasium to watch Press's players try to do things with a ball that Pete had mastered long before he hit puberty. Give Pete Maravich an old gym, a YMCA cage where he could practice his shooting, ballhandling, dribbling, and passing, and all the world's troubles would temporarily disappear. Basketball and thoughts of basketball were his home away from home, even when he was home.

❧❧

Veteran network television college-basketball analyst **BILLY PACKER** *cut his basketball teeth on the Atlantic Coast Conference, where he played basketball at Wake Forest. Packer was one of a number of ACC players who spent many summers at Campbell College in Buie's Creek, North Carolina, taking part in a*

summer basketball camp that featured a skinny little
kid whose dad, Press Maravich, was one of the camp's
longtime coaches:

The first time I ever saw Pete was when I was in college and
his dad was coaching at Clemson. He was just a kid, probably in grade school at the time, and he would come to our
practices or shoot-arounds and kind of get in the way doing
things like dribbling between his legs. He was tiny then and
the ball was big to his hands, yet he was incredibly gifted.
We used to think how it was such a shame that the kid was
never going to have any size to him because he's so fun to
watch. And he was a real cocky little guy.

❦

MARAVICH, *on his first experience with the game, as a*
toddler in West Virginia:

As soon as I was old enough, though the ball was half my
size, I began dribbling constantly in the gym, acquiring a
skill for bouncing the ball on a wooden surface.[1]

❦

BILL TROTT, *one of the established starters at*
Raleigh, North Carolina's Needham-Broughton High
School when Maravich transferred there before his
junior year, had actually met Maravich several years
earlier at the Campbell College camp:

He was obviously an incredible talent. I had seen him at
Campbell College when I was about twelve years old. I
remember Pete as being a hotdog, someone who could dribble behind his back and spin the ball on his finger. But to be
perfectly honest he didn't impress me much at the time as
much of an athlete. I thought he was more of a skinny, gym-
rat kind of a kid. I still had the same impression of him when
he moved to Raleigh. He had a very good shot, but it was

very unorthodox, too. He hadn't quite gotten strong enough in his legs to get off a good jump shot. His best shot at the beginning of the year was more like a set shot.

Yet he eventually succeeded so well because he had that inner confidence as well as a sense of showmanship in him. He probably overachieved because of his confidence. He was willing to try the hard pass or take the hard shot when other people gave up too quickly with those things because they didn't succeed the first or second time trying to do it. Pete was unbelievably creative, even though he was not enamored of playing defense. I didn't realize I was playing with a (basketball) genius while I was playing with him. That realization didn't hit me until I saw him playing in college and the pros.

⁂

MARAVICH, *on his learning the game's intricacies at an early age:*

I couldn't get enough basketball. When dad was coaching the Clemson team, I was there. When he went to scout a team, I was there watching every move and listening to every word. We were married to our sport, and together we continued to grow in knowledge of what basketball could be. I was so close to Dad in his study of the game that he began treating me as if I were an assistant coach. At age thirteen, I identified plays and patterns and made suggestions to Dad as to how he should devise defenses to combat certain offenses, and vice versa. I became a real student of basketball, and this was just the beginning.[2]

⁂

MARAVICH, *on his willingness as a youth to try almost anything to test and improve his ballhandling skills:*

One night during a thunderstorm, I awoke, got out of bed, and walked to the window to watch the rain pelt the backyard with huge drops. As the wind swirled the rain across

Maravich was a junior when he transferred into Needham-Broughton High School in Raleigh, North Carolina, to become the only underclassman among the team's starting five.

the grass, the lightning illuminated the puddles forming on our muddy basketball court. The temptation was too much for me. I forced open my bedroom window and crawled out into the downpour. In my bare feet I ran to the muddied ground and began to dribble. The water splashed and the mud splattered the legs of my pajamas as I bounced the ball between my legs and behind my back. After several minutes, I stopped dribbling and lifted the ball toward the sky watching the rain cleanse mud from it. A huge smile curled across my lips, for I knew if I could dribble under these circumstances, I would have no problem on the basketball court.[3]

〰〰

Another of Maravich's acquaintances in Raleigh was
BOB SANDFORD, *who had also met the Pistol-to-be at*
summer camp and later became one of Pete's best
friends:

When I was fifteen, I attended basketball camp at Campbell
College, and I know Pete was thirteen because I was two
years older than him. Pete was way ahead of his age group,
so they moved him up to the older group to play with us. We
became friends right off the bat. We just kind of hit it off. I
later went on to play college ball at a small school in Virginia
and would then come back home to Raleigh to work summers at the YMCA. Pete would come up there and shoot all
day long and play around while I worked. Then he would go
nap for a while and play in a men's league at night.

It was a real good summer league that included some
guys who had played at N.C. State, North Carolina, and
Wake Forest. I was living with three other guys in an apartment in the summertime. Pete practically lived there. He
would sleep on the couch. We were a couple years older
than him, and we just kind of looked out for him.

〰〰

Maravich wasn't a total stranger among his peers when
he later went on to play at LSU. One of his future
Tigers teammates was **TOMMY HESS,** *who, like Pete,*
was born in Pennsylvania and attended the Campbell
College summer basketball camp:

I grew up in a small coal-mining town in western Pennsylvania called Portage. We first met at the basketball camp at
Campbell College, right outside of Raleigh. I was eight or
nine years old, meaning Pete must have been eleven or
twelve because he's three years older than me. My dad was a
counselor there and had a room right off of the main gym, a
janitor's room, so I slept there in a bunk bed with my dad.

I was a little nervous and edgy because it was really my first time away from home. By the evening of my first day at camp, word was already flowing throughout the camp about Pete. I'll never forget it. After the evening meal, the counselors—college guys working the camp—would scrimmage for about an hour, and the campers could go to the main gym to watch. Guys like Billy Packer and Len Chappell were among those who played in those games.

Well, here's Pistol Pete who's about twelve years old, and he's out there playing with these older guys, and that in itself is an amazing story. Physically, he couldn't run up and down the court like they could, but as far as his ballhandling skills and his shooting, he could hold his own, and right away I fell in love with the guy. I always thought I was a good ballhandler, and I was, and I was a good passer—I had great vision—but this guy was something different.

I used a good basic bounce pass, but with him there was no telling where you would get the ball from. Intimidating? No. It made me want to do the same things he did. I remember him being there and actually helping to teach ballhandling and dribbling skills. He would always demonstrate, but it wasn't done in such a way that Press was trying to show him off. He was doing things we had never seen or tried to experiment with, but that's what you go to camp for, and that helped bring creativity to my own game.

∞∞∞

Pete's first head coach at Needham-Broughton High School in Raleigh was **OLIN BROADWAY,** *who had played college ball at Wake Forest and whose younger brother, Jimmy, was one of Pete's teammates during Maravich's junior year at the school. By this time, Press Maravich had already been in Raleigh for one year as assistant coach at North Carolina State, having moved ahead as his wife, Helen, and Pete stayed back for one more year in Clemson, South Carolina:*

What I remember in seeing him as a young kid was that he was a terrific foul shooter. When you saw him in those days when he was a teenager at the camp, he was six feet two inches and if he weighed 130 pounds I would have been surprised. He was not particularly fast, but he just had that court moxie that few players ever got. He just kind of knew where everybody was. He could pass the ball well and had a sense of what everybody else on the court was doing at any one time, and he could shoot the basketball, of course. When he came to Broughton, he immediately stepped into the starting lineup.

We played a few games and Pete did well—his junior year, which was my brother's senior year. We played some really tough nonleague teams early in the season, and I think we started out with a 3-2 record. We really started winning as we got into the season, and one of the games that got us over the hump was at New Hanover High School in Wilmington, North Carolina, where a coach by the name of Leon Brogben, the Johnny Wooden of North Carolina high school basketball, was nearing his retirement. He had won seven state championships in eight years playing in the state's highest classification. Broughton High School had lost something like twelve straight on their court, although we had beaten them at our place the year before with a rigged defense that they couldn't figure out.

I knew Brogben as being very fundamental, meaning he would run a lot of man-to-man defense. He had a big six-seven kid who was barrel-chested, but I imagined that he would not be particularly agile. So when the game started, we had one play in our game plan. I asked our guards to cross out front. They were Pete and Billy Trott, an ideal teammate for Pete because he was a good ballhandler and totally unselfish—he loved to see Pete score. Meanwhile, my brother Jimmy was playing in the center position with the big guy on him. We had the forwards on one side, a very simple play, setting a short pick inside. Jimmy was supposed to swing around the pick and then get the ball twelve feet

Parents of the Needham-Broughton High School boys basketball team gather for
Spirit Night. Maravich's parents, Helen and Press, are the tenth and eleventh
parents pictured, going from left to right. Jimmy Broadway's parents, Frances and
Olin, are at the far left in the photo.

from the basket. If we got him that close we knew he could shoot a jump shot unless the guy came out and lunged at him, at which time Jimmy could fake him and probably draw the foul. It was a play that required a lot of timing—the ball had to arrive in Jimmy's hands at just the right moment because we didn't want the big center to have time to recover before Jimmy got the ball.

Pete was dishing it off just about as perfectly as could be. First time we ran it, we got one foul on the big guy. We came down the next time and ran it again, and now we had two fouls on him. So they sat him on the bench, and didn't bring him back until the beginning of the second quarter. We ran the play again and now we had three fouls on the big guy, putting him back on the bench for the rest of the first half. He was back in to open the second half, so we ran the same play and now he had four fouls on him. It was unbelievable. Brogben put him on the bench and we had an eight-point lead at that point.

Ultimately, Brogben decided at the beginning of the fourth quarter that he had to throw everything he had at us, so he put the big guy back in. By that point Pete had five points, but when you understand how skilled he was at giving the ball off, you had to give him a lot of credit for what he had done up to that point. Brogben decided if he was going to do anything, and by then we were ahead by twelve points, he pulled the press out and that was ideal. Pete ate it alive and ended up the game with something like thirty-five points, and he also gave the ball up four or five times. That was our first real outward sign that Pete was going to be a really spectacular basketball player.

Maravich's move to Broughton wasn't as silky smooth as one of his between-the-leg dribbles or behind-the-back passes. As a new kid on the block and a junior, he was about to crack the lineup of a team that had five seniors back, all expecting to start, and a youngster by the name of Ed Parker was odd man out when Maravich worked his way into the starting lineup. One of those other seniors was BILL TROTT, the team's point guard:

We were probably pretty tough on him moving him because we had an all-senior team coming back that was pretty good. It was a hard thing to break into, but he broke into it and did very well. He also played on the tennis team, although he was not nearly as interested in tennis as he was in basketball. One of the things I remember about him was when after practice, he would go to halfcourt and consistently make three out of five shots from there by throwing the ball up in the air and having it hit the floor around the foul line and banking it in. It sounds so incredible I hesitate to tell people about it, but I saw him do it a number of times. Every now and then I could make one, but he would make at least 50 percent of them by bouncing them in.

✽✽✽

TROTT and his teammates took to Maravich fairly quickly and befriended him, even if he really wasn't one of the crowd in all respects:

Pete would carry a basketball around with him everywhere. For kids that age, it wasn't cool to be carrying a basketball around with them all the time, but Pete didn't care about appearing cool. He would even bounce the ball out of his car when his mother drove along the street. I don't know how he did that because he couldn't control the speed of the car, and she might have speeded up and slowed down.

Pete had a nice personality, a kind of goofiness, and I don't mean in a derogatory sense. He may even have been a little nerdy, perhaps the Bill Gates of basketball in his time. He had a high level of energy, almost like nervous energy. He was always goofing around and cutting up, and maybe that was a cover-up for how serious and dedicated he truly was about basketball, and he was single-minded in his dedication to basketball. Everything else in life, including schoolwork, he took very lightly. That was in contrast to how I saw him a week before he died, which was mature and serious.

✽✽✽

Although BILLY PACKER didn't see Pete Maravich play basketball year-round, he saw enough of him over the summers at Campbell College to keep tabs on Pete's gradual development both physical and in his basketball prowess. The former took longer than the latter:

When he was young, Pete had a great reputation as a ball-handler. But he was still small, and obviously very, very thin. I remember going to the East-West All-Star Game when Pete was a senior in high school and watching him set a scoring record for that game. Pete was probably six-four and a half then and weighed something like 145, and at that time a lot of Division I coaches didn't feel he would be a great star on a good team in college. Because he didn't have the necessary college boards score to get into the ACC at the time, he went to a prep school (Edwards Military Academy in Salemburg, North Carolina). In the year he was there they had an outstanding team, and Pete continued to score extremely well.

By then it had become obvious that he would be a heck of a college player. He got up to about six-six and was no longer skinny and weak. That year of prep school pulled him into the upper echelons as not only a player but also a prospect.

By the time he finished his freshman year at LSU and came back to Campbell College that summer, you realized at that point that this guy was one of the great players in the country. It was interesting to watch him move from a five-foot-seven, 100-pound ninth grader to a six-foot-six, 185-pound prep schooler to what he eventually became at LSU, where you practically couldn't hurt him because he was so wiry.

From the time he was a junior in high school to when he graduated from college, the standard fare for him was at least a box and one. Many times, the triangle and two was also used, and there was always a feeling you could get physical with him because he was so lean, but he was also incredibly conditioned. Because he got boxed and one so much, he had to learn how to move without the ball in order to get it back. He would normally get it on the in-bounds, but then he would have to give it up and work like crazy to get it back, and he had great instincts as to how to do that. And let's face it, when you score over forty points a game for three years in a row and you are the offensive threat on your team in a very good league, you've got to know how to move without the ball some.

❧❧❧

As much as Pete loved basketball for the thrill of competition and testing out new skills, the court was also a refuge for him, his comfort zone many hours a day, as his Raleigh lifetime-buddy-to-be **BOB SANDFORD** *found out:*

When Pete stepped onto a basketball court, he was in his own world. But off the basketball court, he wasn't too confident. He was kind of shy growing up. He didn't have a lot of social skills, which is kind of why he took up with us because we knew about everyone, and everywhere we went he went with us, tagging along like a little brother. He was an easy guy to talk to, and once you made a friendship with him, it was a long-lasting friendship. But he didn't take to everybody. If you hit it off good, then he was your friend for a long time. After he became very popular—an all-American and that kind of stuff—people were always trying to get a piece on him: Sign this or be a spokesman for that. People were always trying to use him, so he was very cautious of people.

❦

As the prodigal son of the hometown North Carolina State basketball coach, Maravich could have been a real pain for his first Broughton coach, **OLIN BROADWAY,** *but Broadway found the opposite to be true. For as much of a hot dog as Maravich was, he pretty much deferred to his coaches, at least in high school and college:*

Pete was about as coachable as any kid I've ever seen. He was sincere, genuine, wanted to win, and wanted his teammates to score, and if you had a game plan, he would run it to perfection. If you didn't have a game plan, he'd do what he usually did best and that was shoot. I think even in the pros he got into that situation where the coach didn't coach very much and just kind of threw the ball out on the court and let the guys play. And when a coach does that, Pete would shoot a lot.

Pete was smart, but he took coaching very well. Something happened one day on the court just as a practice was ending. I heard somebody swear. It wasn't very loud and it was obvious it wasn't meant to be heard. But I did hear it, and Pete looked up at me and said, "Coach, I'm sorry, I shouldn't have done that." I said, "Well, Pete, what I want you to do is stay after practice and run sprints until I tell you to stop." "Yes, sir." And he did.

I never got any feedback from Press that I was utilizing Pete wrong, nor did I get any feedback from Pete that he didn't like what I was doing. There was no attempt to coach or to use any different-level knowledge. A little later, when Pete was in the pros, he was kidding me one day when he said, "Coach, remember those loose-ball drills we used to run? They don't let me do them now." I said, "Right, Pete, but somewhere along the line you have to learn how to get the loose balls." And he said, "Right, but now they're paying me so many million dollars that they're afraid I would get hurt running the loose-ball drills." But he was pulling my leg a little bit because we *had* run loose-ball drills.

At Broughton, Maravich was a big fish in a big pond, quickly standing out as a charismatic basketball star in a school of two thousand students in an affluent, predominantly white part of Raleigh, as basketball and tennis teammate BILL TROTT, now a Raleigh attorney, explains:

It was a real good high school in those days. But Pete didn't dedicate himself to schoolwork. The reason why he went to prep school was because he couldn't meet the minimum on the college boards—an ACC rule, and I heard that one of the reasons his father took the job at LSU was because the SEC didn't have such a rule. He wanted Pete to play for him, and Pete wanted to play for his father, yet he couldn't legally get into N.C. State where his father was coaching.

They eventually declared that 800 rule unconstitutional, but that's what went on in those days.

Pete was one of those guys who was tall, outgoing, and with a quick smile on his face who would speak to people while walking down the halls. Still, I never thought of him being cocky or anything like that. He just liked to be nice to people. It was a big school. It must have been hard to come into a school that size as an eleventh grader and break into a basketball team, but he did it. He was pretty much one-dimensional in his love for basketball and I don't remember him having any interest in dating. In tennis, he was kind of gangly, even though he had a good touch. He was all arms and legs going around the tennis court.

❦

MARAVICH, on dealing with the pressure of being his team's star player, starting his senior year at Needham-Broughton, after he had grown to six-foot-four between his junior and senior seasons:

I was the only returning starter from a 19-4 team. The responsibility fell upon me to be the leader of an inexperienced team. It seemed when I was hot, the team was hot, and when I cooled off for a time, the team seemed to follow suit. Though I was averaging thirty-two points per game, the weight of responsibility at times annoyed me, and I remember letting Dad know about it.[4]

❦

During the summer between Pete's sophomore and junior years of high school, there was still some uncertainty among the basketball players at Needham-Broughton that Maravich was finally going to join his dad in Raleigh and thus transfer into their school. One of the first indications that Pete was making the move that summer came when he started showing up at the

PHOTO COURTESY OF JIMMY BROADWAY

The Needham-Broughton Caps welcomed Pete into their fold prior to the 1963-64 season. From left to right are teammates Jimmy Broadway (No. 45), Dickie Smith (No. 51), Doug Bridges (No. 55), Maravich, Steve Horney (No. 33), and Billy Trott (No. 21). Coach Olin Broadway is kneeling in front.

Raleigh YMCA where his teammates-to-be, such as **JIMMY BROADWAY**, loved to play ball:

After finally meeting him, I would make arrangements with him to get to the Y at eight o'clock in the morning and play all day long. He wore me out. However, he would periodically get tired and he'd have to sit down and catch his breath. And I would think, *Gosh, he works out all the time, why does he need to go out?* As we now know, maybe the heart wasn't working the way it should have. We also played in the Y league with a mix of high school and college players. Pete was scoring like fifty points a game and I was struggling to get twenty-five. You had some good competition and good games, and Pete was shooting the lights out of it. We built a good friendship at this time, and when school started we didn't have any problem with Pete being there. Pete took Ed

Parker's place as a starter and that might have bothered Ed a little bit, but I never noticed it. We ended up losing at Greensboro in double overtime in the state playoffs. As it turns out, Pete never won a championship, and he even referred to that as one his team could have won.

One Saturday morning, we had just finished practicing and he asked me to rebound for him on foul shots and he said, "I'm not going to quit until I miss." It was like 178 shots later that he missed one and we went home . . . and he was just messing around. As well as I got to know Pete, I never stepped inside the front door of his house. I remember knocking on the door and he would always come to the door, but I never would go in. I saw his mother one time. Then his mother came to Parents Night and those are the only two times I ever saw her, and I don't think I ever spoke to her. He didn't even talk about his whole life. I can't tell you much about what he did talk about other than basketball.

We used to play H-O-R-S-E all the time. He had this one particular move he could do without walking where he would go through his legs, around his waist, spin it off his finger, and bounce it off his forehead and score. I could never get that one. I heard he did that one year in practice after I left, but that goes along with his ballhandling ability. Spinning the ball from one finger to the other and going around his waist spinning the ball on his finger. I also saw him play in the East-West All-Star Game. He scored in the forties. They were going to win the game late and he was just messing around while he was deep in the left corner and falling out of bounds. Right then he throws up a right-handed hook shot and he hits it. He just punctuated what he had been doing all night. The next time I saw him was when he was playing at Edwards Military Academy. It was amazing how he had grown from being a wet-behind-the-ears young guy to where he was almost a grown man. Had grown about two or more inches and put on twenty or thirty pounds and was wearing a mustache.

One thing funny about Pete: He never took showers with us after the game. He thought it would affect his muscles and somehow alter them.

❦

SANDFORD and Maravich stayed in close touch with each other after high school. During the summers between their college years, with Pete at LSU and Sandford playing for a small college in Virginia, Pete would return to Raleigh and share an apartment with Sandford. That was their base camp from which they went out and took part in various basketball camps, and it also gave Pete an opportunity to give birth to a memorable personal tradition:

We became tremendous friends over the years. The floppy socks he wore were my socks. One day we were going to play and he didn't have any socks, just a pair of shoes. This was the summer before he went to LSU. We were getting ready to go play somewhere and he said he needed some socks, so I told him to get some socks out of my drawer. I had these old gray socks that I wore to work every day with my coaching shoes, and had six or seven pairs in there, and two or three of them were about worn out.

For some reason, he put some white socks on with a pair of those old gray socks over them and then would go play. He had a real good game and he was talking about it and I said, "Man, the only reason you had a good game was because you had a pair of my old socks on." He said, "You know how those socks lay down on my shoes"—you know, he had about size-fourteen shoes—"these socks make my feet look smaller." A couple of days later, we went to play again and he put the old socks on and had another good game. When he left to go back to school, he went through my drawers and took three or four pairs. Every summer, he would go through my drawer and get my old ones. He didn't want my good ones. And he wore them through all of his career.

Even when he was all grown up, Maravich loved coming back to visit his old stomping grounds in North Carolina. Here he is getting ready to head home after visiting his good buddy Bob Sandford in Raleigh. Although Pistol Pete was a wizard with a basketball, packing plans for car trunks were another story.

Between his senior year at Needham-Broughton and his arrival at LSU, Maravich spent a year at Edwards Military Academy, a prep school, in Salemburg, North Carolina, further honing his basketball skills while going about the more important task of working to improve his SAT scores, which a year earlier had kept him out of playing basketball in the ACC. **LES ROBINSON**, who had played for Pete's dad, Press, at North Carolina State and was now coaching under Press at his alma mater, remembers the first time that he drove Pete back to Edwards on a Sunday night after having spent the weekend back in Raleigh hanging around with his dad and the N.C. State team:

Press was my mentor, and because of that I was around Pete a lot. I was the freshman coach at N.C. State. I would take Pete back to school on Sunday nights during his prep year at what was then known as Edwards Military Academy. The first time I did that Coach Maravich warned me, "He's going to fight you when he gets down there." Pete was kind of a hardheaded young man and I was only twenty-one or twenty-two years old, so I was just a college guy to him. I was more like a big brother than a coach.

When we got down there, I could see it was a rough place in the sense that the buildings were old and dilapidated. He didn't want to get out of the car, saying he was sick of the place. So, just like Press had said, he started fighting me about it. I said, "You're going and that's it." I almost physically had to get him to go back. Now while he was a heckuva basketball player, he wasn't very strong. I was only about six feet tall, but I weighed about 190 pounds. Finally he said, "I want you to go upstairs and see this room." So I helped him carry his bags up there to his third-floor room, and it was bad. It was hard for me to lie. He had a rope out of his room. I figured he had it there so that he could sneak out, but he said, "I've got it here because my dad told me to put it here for in case there was ever a fire."

∞∞∞

MARAVICH, *on attending prep school:*

After graduation Dad and I decided I should attend prep school for a year before subjecting myself to a college basketball program and the rigors of university level academics. My preoccupation with basketball had affected my performance in the classroom. Dad suggested Edwards Military Academy in Salemburg, North Carolina, as a warm-up before college life, and Mom agreed.

I had grown to six-foot-four, but Dad knew I would be beaten physically if he pushed me on into college and I went up against players on the university level, especially in the highly competitive Atlantic Coast Conference. Again, Dad was correct in his judgment. Edwards helped put a little more strength in my body, as well as discipline me some more in the classroom. The basketball program was also a plus. We were a fast-break-oriented team.[5]

❦

When Maravich was in high school, prep athletes didn't get anywhere near the amount of national attention they now get in publications such as USA Today and over the Internet. Maravich did make Parade Magazine's high school all-American team in 1965 following his senior year at Needham-Broughton, but other than that he was pretty much an unknown outside of the South. Veteran national high school writer **DAVE KRIDER,** *who was USA Today's national high school writer for several years, has been covering high school sports out of his Indiana home for almost forty years, and he offers a brief media history lesson on how and why a player of Maravich's magnitude could go virtually unnoticed even while averaging more than thirty points for one of the biggest high schools in a state that is a basketball hotbed:*

What they had back then was *Parade Magazine* at the end of the year, and I think *Street and Smith's* had just barely started their high school coverage around that time, and all that was was a list of names. When I went into the business in '61, there was nothing on high school sports on a national basis. People were interested in their county and possibly their state, but nobody thought in national terms at all. Everything I'd see that had anything about high school sports after that I'd grab it up and keep it, so I have stack upon stack of stuff that has come out over the years. Jim O'Brien had a high school teacher in Pittsburgh who started compiling lists for him. Then he gave it to me and I did it for twenty-one years, and then I went full-time with *USA Today.*

Even with *Street and Smith's* getting into high school coverage, you had to have the pages for their basketball issue prepared at the beginning of the summer, after which you would get late transfers that would change team ratings. You could get a player like Michael Jordan who came out of nowhere and didn't even get into the magazine because we learned about him in late July, and the high school stuff was already wrapped up by that time. He never got in *Street and Smith's* at all and that turned out to be one of his biggest disappointments. When Michael was in his mid- to late twenties and met O'Brien at a banquet, he said to O'Brien, "You know that one of my biggest disappointments was not getting into *Street and Smith's,*" which of course was a preseason magazine. Even as an NBA scoring champ at the time, he was pretty crushed that he had never been in *Street and Smith's* magazine. It was the preseason Bible and if you made that it meant a lot to the kids. We just found out about him too late.

Maravich was in the *Parade* Sunday supplement, and he was one of the featured guys among the forty or so kids that are picked, and that was the first that I had heard of Pete Maravich. I started writing high school sports on a national basis in 1970 for *Letterman Magazine*. That was the first national high school sports magazine ever put out and it lasted five years. It never made a profit, but it was a wonderful magazine.

❈

Even though there were no Street and Smith's *preseason high school all-American teams as far back as the mid-sixties, there are memories and testimonials about great players of that pre-media era. None of those remembrances pay homage to a high school player's skills as well as the story that current N.C. State athletic director* **LES ROBINSON** *tells in recalling one day with high school senior Pete Maravich in December 1964:*

While celebrating the fiftieth and last year of Reynolds Coliseum (during the 1998–99 season), a writer asked me a good question. At the time all this stuff was being written about the greatest team ever and the greatest player ever and all that kind of stuff, and this guy says to me, "Les, tell me the greatest performance that you saw and which nobody ever really saw in this building." I didn't even have to think long. It was December 1964, and the year of that team at N.C. State that under Press went on that year to win the ACC championship.

It just so happened that nine of the twelve N.C. State players that season were married. Because of that, we played our last game sometime around December 20, and the team was free to go home for Christmas. Many of us, however, including three players who had wives who worked, stayed around and didn't have anything to do but play basketball. So we played three-on-three one day a couple days before Christmas. The six players consisted of four of the N.C. State starters, myself, and Pete. We played three-on-three for a good three hours. We mixed the sides up and just kept playing.

When you're playing three-on-three, there's not a lot of help there, and there's a lot of one-and-one play, and a lot of give and go. Well, when Pete Maravich had that much of the floor to work with, forget about it. It was bad enough when you had *five* players on the floor trying to play him. And he was *a senior in high school*. When the rest of us went down to our lockers, Pete went home. The other five of us had lockers down there, and one of those was Pete Coker, who had transferred in from Dartmouth.

We were sitting there all worn out because we had played forever. And Pete (Coker) says, "Les, that's the greatest performance that I have ever seen. I have never seen a greater player than what we just saw today." Pistol Pete beat those guys like a drum. A senior in high school— ballhandling, passing, shooting, driving . . . his game was just on that day. I had played with Jerry West a lot and played ACC basketball and been around a lot of great players. I had also played in a tournament in West Virginia where most of the great players had played—Russell, West, Robertson, Lucas, Havlicek. They all played in it. My dad had started it in the forties. So I had been around a lot of great players and performances, and I had never seen anything like what I saw from Pete that day. I'd pay good money to have a video of it.

I played a lot of one-on-one with Pete, and that was a joke. I loved doing it because he was so great. He would play with anybody that played with him. He just loved to play so much. That was in the days when there was one pro game on TV every week, on Sunday, and usually it seemed it was Wilt versus Russell. Or sometimes West and Baylor. When that game was over, Pete would come out to married housing where we lived and try to get someone to go play with him. He wanted to go out there and emulate the moves he had just seen. He would beg people to play.

When he and I played, we played possession—you keep the ball as long as you keep making shots. He wasn't great defensively at this stage because he was so weak, so if you played possession you could occasionally get hot and go on to win. The whole key was not giving up the ball. Just like playing pool. He's the only player I could play against who, when he dribbled the ball, he would dribble high and get you to lean to try and get it, and he'd go around you one way or the other. He'd tease you out there with it and when you leaned to go get it, the ball would just disappear on you and he'd be by you. I look back and go, "My goodness. He was good." You knew how good he was.

DAVE KRIDER *at first knew nothing about Maravich other than what he had read in* **Parade Magazine,** *but he made it a point to find out more, and the more he found out the more he was amazed, even astonished:*

I loved Pete Maravich. I still have the *Sports Illustrated* cover that had about five different poses of him including one with his dad, and that's probably my all-time favorite *SI* cover. He was, arguably, the greatest showman college basketball ever had. Looking at the (*Parade*) magazine, I see him with a crew cut and looking very babyfaced in it. He was a first-teamer from Broughton High School in Raleigh, North Carolina. It says, "Son of North Carolina State coach Press Maravich. Had a fabulous year. Lowest point production (in a) game was eighteen. Went over forty-three times. Led team in assists in addition to scoring." Quote: "No high school basketball player in my era of covering sports has created as much furor as Pete Maravich," says *Raleigh Times* sports editor Bruce Phillips. Listed at six-foot-four. By the way, Lew Alcindor was on that team, too.

It's hard to say high-school-wise where he would have rated because I didn't know much about his high school career. Obviously, college-wise, though, he was one of the greatest showmen and one of the greatest scorers. I can remember then as a sports editor of a small paper I could still get tickets to almost any game if I wrote far enough ahead of time. So one year, and I can't remember if it was Pete's junior or senior year at LSU, a friend of mine, Norm Scharf, and I decided to drive (from LaPorte, Indiana) down to Kentucky to see Pete Maravich play. Now this was a 750-mile roundtrip. We drive down one afternoon and night, and he dropped me off at work at 6:00 A.M. the next day so we could see Pete play Kentucky at Lexington. I think he had about forty-five or forty-six points that night.

The thing I remember most about that night was his crashing right into the press table right in front of me while trying to get a loose ball. This was in the first half, and he really banged himself up badly. Norm was sitting in front of me under the table, which was underneath one of the baskets, because he had gotten a pass as a photographer. We both just about got knocked out. Pete hurt his knee but played the whole second half, and still got all those points. I think that was the only time I ever got to see him play live, and I had to pay for it by not getting any sleep that night so I could get back and put out the sports pages that day. But it was well worth it.

∞∞∞

Many people long assumed that when it came time for Pete to play college basketball, he would go play for his father regardless of where Press happened to be coaching at the time, and that is the way it worked out. But such an arrangement wasn't necessarily a given to Pete, as LES ROBINSON *recalls:*

West Virginia was recruiting him, and Pete liked West Virginia. Bucky Walters was coaching there. Hot Rod Hundley was there. So was Jerry West. I remember talking to Pete about it right after Press had taken the LSU job—and he had wanted to take me there with him, but part of his deal was that he had to keep both assistant coaches there.

One weekday morning Pete came walking through the house while Press and I were just talking. The phone rang and it was for Pete. Bucky Walters. They talked for about fifteen or twenty minutes back in another room, and then Pete walked back through, and Press said, "What did Bucky have to say?" "Oh, he was just talking about West Virginia. It sounds good." So Press says, "West Virginia, my a—. You're not going to West Virginia." Pete said, "I told you, I'm not going down to LSU unless I get a car."

Pete was one recruit who could get a car legally, and Press said, "Car, my a—." Well, the next year I was coaching at a small high school in Florida and we were talking about the scouting schedule in mid-October. Coach Maravich would talk very openly with me, to include what his salary was and other stuff like that. He was telling me one time about all his financial hardships. He didn't have a secretive bone in his body. And I told him, "Well, I guess you're enjoying that new big salary." He told me he had signed a five-year deal for $15,000 a year, and he said, "Hell, no, I've got a huge mortgage—we got a bigger house than we should have—and I've got two car payments." And I said, "*Two* car payments?!" And he said, "Yeah, I got Pete a car." It was that little Volkswagen, but it was legal because he had bought it himself. And as we all know, Pete ended up going to LSU to play for his dad.

2

TIGER TOWN

Anyone with enough knowledge of basketball history to know who Pete Maravich was might think that he was a drawling, born-and-bred Southerner who was the ultimate rebel by forsaking football and friends to play that strange off-season sport of basketball at LSU. It would be easy to think of Maravich in that revisionist-history sort of way, considering that he became an overnight national sensation at LSU, averaging more than forty points a game as a sophomore playing for his dad in a program that had long paled beside LSU's potent football tradition.

But Maravich was by no means a prototypical Southern genteelman, at least not the kind who sauntered slowly from place to place, perhaps with a chaw or toothpick in the side of his mouth. He was actually Yankee born and bred, having been born in Pennsylvania, a fairly fast-talking and slightly high-pitched slicker raised by a dad who was a native Northerner through and through.

In coming to Baton Rouge, where petrochemical plants and transplanted Mississippians mix in a community colored

LSU SPORTS INFORMATION DEPARTMENT

A rare photo indeed: Pete in his LSU days without the floppy socks and not in the act of shooting.

by a live-and-let-live mentality, Maravich was heading into a part of the country where segregation was still in full swing. And that's not a reference to football players on one side of the gymnasium and basketball players on the other. Whites had their own high school basketball conferences and the blacks had theirs. Southeastern Conference athletics were still pretty much lily-white, which assured SEC basketball at least second-tier status in the world of national collegiate athletics.

In a sense, Maravich was black and white. His vast street-sense basketball skills were Harlem-Globetrotterish and yet his heritage was very much Caucasian. His basketball wizardry helped reduce the gap between those two worlds. Pete's coaching dad, Press Maravich, preceded his son to LSU by a year as Pete tacked on an extra year of secondary schooling at Edwards Military Academy, before heading to Louisiana to join his dad for a four-year era of unprecedented showmanship basketball that ended with Pete scoring 3,667 points while averaging more than forty-four points a game—both NCAA records that still stand and appear as unbreakable as Joe DiMaggio's fifty-six-game hitting streak.

Remember, this was in the days before billion-dollar TV contracts, Dick Vitale, seemingly hourly ESPN coverage, and lottery draft picks raking in a king's ransom. In a very real sense, Maravich's four-year stint at LSU had a part in all those things becoming a reality a decade or two later. Oh, and the three thousand–plus points? Maravich accomplished all that in just three seasons. Freshmen weren't eligible to play varsity college basketball in those days.

MARAVICH, *on his arrival at LSU in the fall of 1966:*

When I came to town, there were no brass bands and no ticker tape. Football was in the air; and as far as Louisiana was concerned, that was all that mattered. The basketball team practiced unnoticed in the high school gymnasium.[1]

Being Pete Maravich didn't carry with it an exemption from a little bit of freshman hazing, as fellow incoming freshman basketball player **RANDY LAMONT,** *who roomed with Maravich their freshman year, points out:*

At LSU, when we went there, everyone had hours. All the girls had to be in by eleven on weekdays and one on weekends. Our dates normally started at like seven o'clock, where now they don't even start thinking about going out until ten or so. We had blind dates. We would ask the older guys on the teams who had dates to try and get us a date, too. We'd go out dancing, partying, movies, or whatever there was to do.

As freshmen, especially, we didn't have girls hanging out with the basketball players. It was still a military school then and all the freshmen had to shave their heads. I'm talking like taking a pair of clippers and cutting it as close as you can, although not actually shaving it. It was the same for all the freshman guys. Plus you had to wear a purple-and-gold beanie that had a little yellow bill on it that you turned up and it had "Dawg" and your last name. And if you didn't shave your head, then some of the upperclassmen would take care of that for you. So you were better off doing it yourself by getting a teammate or friend to do it for you. Then for the first football game, you had to go in your pajamas and then had to stand up until LSU scored its first touchdown, then you could sit down. That made it kind of interesting.

So there weren't a lot of girls looking at freshman guys, at least not until their hair grew out. This may have been something the upperclassmen started themselves just so they would have first pick with girls, I don't know. Once it grew back, then you could keep it. Pete in his crew cut looked just like all the rest of us—stupid. Kind of like Knucklehead Smith, I guess, just like the rest of us. As freshmen, he was cool, but all that stuff didn't happen until after we started playing basketball. Up until then, we all looked like stupid, bald freshmen without too much going for us at that point.

We were there over the holidays when everybody else was gone, to practice Thanksgiving and Christmas. During Mardi Gras when everybody else got off, we were there practicing. It really came together after the first couple of weeks of practices when we could see what he was doing. There were some pretty big basketball fans who would stop by the freshman practice early in the season to see what was going on or what the new crop of players looked like. I heard that one of them stopped by, watched practice for about fifteen or twenty minutes, walked outside, picked up a telephone and called everybody he knew to tell them to get their season tickets now, because they're not going to be available very long.

Pete was a great shot, but his ballhandling was the most terrific thing I had ever seen. He could do things with a basketball that I never even dreamed could be done let alone try to do. We had drills that he and his dad had been doing for years and they had those going on in practice all the time, things like trying to bounce the basketball between your legs in front and catch it behind your back and do it harder and harder until you get that flexibility down. Any number of things to improve your ballhandling.

※※※

Baton Rouge newspaperman **JOE MACALUSO** *was one of a number of journalists-to-be who attended LSU at the same time Maravich was there:*

The entertainment value was terrific. That's what you went to see Pete Maravich for. You never knew what was going to happen next—the blind pass, the spin move, the between-the-legs, the over-the-shoulder pass. You never knew where it was coming from next. It even confused his teammates at times. Jason Williams at Sacramento is the guy now, but he doesn't compare to Pete. Pete showed the way. I was a big Boston Celtic fan in the sixties because I knew who Bill Russell, Bob Cousy, and John Havlicek were. Havlicek was the best sixth man in basketball. Cousy was the best ball-handler around then, but if you go back and watch film, he was good in his times, but he dribbled almost exclusively with his right hand. Maravich was a magician. What he did with a basketball, only the Harlem Globetrotters could come close.

If you know Baton Rouge, there was a subculture here of basketball and had always been. Everyone knew then that Southern University was playing better basketball than LSU and that the black players were better than the white players. There were a lot of players here in the inner-city area that were terrific basketball players, and if you ventured out a little ways you could watch them play. The black people around town knew about Maravich, and they wanted to see him play. In times when the Baton Rouge community could have dissolved into some pretty good racial conflict, sports is probably what kept this place from being a racial powder keg. Maravich probably hastened the arrival of the black player to LSU, not that LSU was the first to crack the egg on that, but he did something to help the black athlete here.

I brought my two brothers up here once to stay with me over Thanksgiving when he was a senior. I had to get them special passes to get them into the game. Afterwards, in the locker room, my brother had a leather jacket on, and they were tagging along behind me. Questions with the media were getting repetitive and Pete was ready to go and it was a holiday weekend, and still he said to me, "Who's that with you?" And I said, "Hey, they're my brothers," and he sat there and talked with these two kids for a couple of minutes, asking them where they're from and thanking them for coming to see the game. He got a pen and signed my brother's jacket, and my brother still has that jacket. My other younger brother gave him the program he had been using to keep score, and Pete signed it across the top "Pistol Pete."

That was the kind of stuff that went unnoticed, that Pete just wanted to be one of the guys. Because he was a celebrity, a superstar, he never could be. He just wanted to be one of the guys. He just wanted to be a basketball player, and in that regard he was a lot like Van Gogh. Van Gogh wanted to be the greatest painter in art history. Maravich was the same way. All he wanted to do was be the best he could be at basketball. When they talk about whatever reason Van Gogh cut his ear off, that was sort of what Pete Maravich did with his life. He turned away from a lot of things for a while, thinking that was the solution. There always seemed to be a different problem as he got a little older. The good thing about him is that when he died, he was at peace with himself and that meant a lot to a lot of people. He was just a different person when I last saw him. That was comforting to see.

⚬⚬⚬⚬

As much as Maravich had filled out during his year at prep school, he still drew some skeptical looks when he arrived at LSU because of his lean, almost fragile-looking frame. **DANNY YOUNG,** *who worked in the LSU sports information office as a student assistant and eventually became good friends with Maravich, recalls those early days in Baton Rouge:*

When I first saw him, I said, "This kid is a basketball player?" He was such a gangly, peculiar-looking thing, but when he got out on that basketball court it didn't take him long to convert people. He could do magic with a basketball. So many experiences I can remember about him, and I'm sure I embellish some of them over the passage of years.

For the freshman games they would pack the Cow Palace, a cow barn basically, where they would put the floor down and play basketball because that's all the importance the university placed on basketball then, and it became standing room only for those freshman games that year. The minute the freshman game was over, the people would get up and leave, and when the varsity came out to warm up everyone was in the process of leaving. It was kind of bad in a way. Usually, Pete was scoring fifty, sixty points a game as a freshman, and everyone was just oohing and ahhing over what he had done. It was just fantastic.

*Soon after Pete Maravich arrived to join his father, Press, there, the coaching dad went to academic adviser **DONALD RAY KENNARD**, now a Louisiana state representative, to get help in finding ways to keep Pete busy when he was away from the basketball court or classroom. Kennard's nickname—X-Ray:*

After we hired Press from North Carolina State, he came to me and said, "X-Ray, you gotta get Pete a job. I don't want him sitting around doing nothing. I want him to do something other than play basketball." So I got him a job. We had had a drugstore called Professional Pharmacy on campus, right behind Tiger Town. Dick Kelly was the owner of the pharmacy. He had played football at Purdue and was a football nut. He was also a basketball nut because he was from Indiana. I called Mr. Kelly and said, "Dick, they got this hotshot coming in here by the name of Pete Maravich. I don't know him, but his father is supposed to meet him this afternoon and I'll bring him over." And he said, "Okay, Poppa, send him over here, but he's going to work like everybody else." He hired a lot of students.

Back then they had home delivery, and kids would ride bikes around campus delivering prescriptions and all. I said, "Pete, you be over at Mr. Kelly's drugstore in the morning. He's going to hire you." About 4:30 that next afternoon, my phone rings and it's Mr. Kelly. He says, "Poppa, I'll tell you what, this is a unique guy you sent over here. His work habits are good, but you'll never guess. . . . This morning when I got to the store to open it up, he was standing there at the door with a foot propped up on the brick wall with a basketball under his arm. So I said, "C'mon in, Pete, give me that basketball and we're going to put it back in the stockroom. You're working eight to five. You get a fifteen-minute break in the morning, an hour break for lunch, and a fifteen-minute break in the afternoon. But the rest of the time, you're going to be stocking this, stocking that, sweeping the floor, whatever.'" Pete says, 'Yes, sir.' At ten o'clock I tell Pete, 'Okay, you've got your break,' and he says, 'Mr. Kelly, can I have my basketball?' He came back behind my counter and got back there by the shelves with his basketball and started in on his drills. He started spinning the ball, dribbling the ball between his legs, etc.

"'Fifteen minutes, time to go to work, Pete.' Basketball goes back on the shelf. . . . 'Twelve o'clock, time for lunch.' 'Can I have my basketball?' Goes out into the parking lot, dribbling around through and behind cars. All that kind of stuff. Then in the afternoon I say, 'Okay, it's three o'clock. Time for a fifteen-minute break.' So then he starts doing a demo with the basketball in the drugstore. Now that ain't bad for business. He did his deal in the drugstore. Got those long aisles and he'd be dribbling down the aisles, going around women trying to get their shampoo or whatever.'"

≈≈≈≈

*Longtime sports media honcho **BUD JOHNSON** had two go-rounds with Pete Maravich, first when he was sports information director at LSU and later when he was the public relations director for the New Orleans Jazz of the NBA, which is where Pete ended up after playing four years for the Atlanta Hawks. Johnson thus saw the Pistol in two different phases of his life, starting as a green freshman at Baton Rouge in 1966–67:*

He was very young and immature when I first met him at LSU. He was very playful and very much wanted to hang out with his buddies and do things with them. After LSU football games, he and his friends Rich Hickman and Jeff Tribbett would go play basketball. While most fraternity boys would be out partying after football games, these guys would be hanging out together and playing pickup basketball.

I recall his years at LSU as his being a very frail athlete who didn't have much stamina. On those weekends when they'd play Saturday-Monday games in the SEC, and you could probably go back, look at the box scores, and see that on Saturday night he's gangbusters against Vanderbilt, and then Monday against Auburn he has a so-so ball game. Putting all the facts together, that heart defect that he had was showing itself to us, but nobody knew it. Considering his heart defect, if he had been a normal human being not playing basketball, he wouldn't have lived to be twenty-one years old. At least, that's what the medical people told me.

Because he took an early interest in sports, specifically basketball, and because he had a daily workout routine that Press prescribed for him, his heart got stronger. Then there's his alcoholism, which he deals with in his book (*Heir to a Dream*). As that progressed, beginning in his college years and continuing in the pros—which, by the way, is a great job for an alcoholic because you work only two hours a day—the alcoholism began to eat away at his heart. So if you say he hadn't been an athlete, he would have died young. But if he hadn't been an alcoholic, he probably would have lived into his seventies. That's the great irony to this whole thing. Again, this is what a medical person told me.

When I first met him, he was about six-four, 165 pounds. He didn't look physically imposing. At least, he didn't look like what the press clippings had made him out to be. No muscle tone. Long arms, long legs. All bones and big eyes. But God, he could handle a basketball. And I asked Press, "Why did you give him all those drills at an early age?" and he said, "Because it gave him confidence. He was always the smallest kid on the team, and it gave him confidence he could do something nobody else could do." And I think Press got caught up in it, because no matter what drill Press had given him, Pete had mastered it by the time Press had gotten home at the end of the day at Clemson or wherever he was going. So he had to come up with something else to challenge Pete. So Press was challenged as well. He was giving him things for finger dexterity and various passes. Nobody else was doing that.

One of my favorite college basketball players was a guy by the name of Dave Bing, who played at Syracuse. Dave happened to be at a summer camp once where Press and Pete were. Pete became fascinated with Dave Bing, so he came home and said, "Daddy, that guy is going to be a great pro player." Press relayed that compliment to Dave Bing, who said, "Coach, your boy is going to be a great pro player," and Pete had to be in high school at the time.

Press was like one of those European gymnasts' coaches. He would coach the same athlete from age five through adulthood. He knew Pete. He knew Pete's strengths and he knew Pete's weaknesses, and he was always giving him something to work on, both in season and out of season. Like Bela Karoyli. In Europe, that's not uncommon. But here was one guy coaching one athlete through much of his adult life. Even after Pete finished playing in the pros, as a tandem, they would go all over Europe putting on clinics.

⚬⚬⚬⚬

Technically speaking, Pete didn't actually play for his father his first season (1966–67) at LSU. His coach was Tigers freshman coach **GREG BERNBROCK,** *who sets the stage for what SEC basketball was like at the time of Pete Maravich's ballyhooed arrival on the scene in the South:*

At that time Kentucky had won the majority of SEC basketball titles. They were legendary under Adolph Rupp, having won four NCAA titles and turned out a ton of professional stars. They had lost the 1965 NCAA finals to Texas Western—now known as Texas–El Paso—but still had produced great talent with guys like Pat Riley and Louie Dampier. Their recruiting was not unlike Notre Dame football—a machine that every year signed great talent to scholarships. Dan Issel was their premier recruit in 1967, the year Pete was a freshman.

To no one's surprise, the other two SEC schools with strong basketball traditions were the two that were geographically closest to the high school basketball talent in the East and Midwest—Vanderbilt and Tennessee. Also, they had arenas that were actually larger than the old Memorial Coliseum at the University of Kentucky. Tennessee's Stokely Center seated something like seventeen thousand and Vandy's gym was comparable in size.

Georgia, Ole Miss, Alabama, and Auburn all had completed or were in the process of building new field houses in 1967. Mississippi State, Florida, and LSU were still using older facilities. While the SEC was still predominantly a football league—especially the seven schools located in Alabama, Florida, Georgia, Louisiana, and Mississippi—basketball interest was on the rise, and Pete Maravich was the catalyst who really took it to the next level and beyond. While the SEC didn't have the depth of strength that the ACC and Big Ten had enjoyed for years, they were beginning to assert themselves, and this showed in intersectional play as well.

⚒

*Maravich's arrival—that was the good news. The bad news, as **BERNBROCK** illustrates, was playing in a home facility built for cowpoking rodeos and scheduling parameters that precluded much in the way of creativity when it came to lining up nonconference opponents:*

Our Ag Center was multipurpose, but primarily for agriculture. They would have some kind of agricultural event in the fall and then another one in February, and we had a portable floor just like the old Boston Garden on which the Celtics played. They put it down on Thanksgiving and usually opened with a weekend game the first weekend in December, so we didn't have a chance to practice in the Ag Center until just a few days before our first home game. The other factor involved was that we had to finish our home schedule by early February because another rodeo or some such was scheduled for mid-February. We were quite restricted as to when we could play in our home facility. So we would start and end our seasons practicing at either University High School or at Catholic High School in Baton Rouge. There also was a limitation on the number of games we could play. I think it might have been twenty-six, which left only five nonconference games after our eighteen-game SEC conference schedule, Tulane home and away, and Loyola (of New Orleans) once. When we could schedule nonconference opponents, we would schedule some of the best teams in the country.

If you count the year we went to the NIT and then the year after Pete graduated, we probably only played about 40 to 45 percent of our games at home, which is pretty remarkable when you think about it. Many programs have long loaded up with patsy schedules in November and December so that they essentially have eight or nine automatic wins before they get to conference play in January. The theory is you get into January at 8-1 or 9-2, split your league games, and, voilà, you come out with a twenty-win season. Press hated that. He wanted to take on all comers because he was smart enough to know that while we might lose a couple more games early on, we would be a heck of a lot better team in the long run.

We had a lot of big wins not only in the SEC but outside the league as well from 1968 through 1971. We won the All-College Tourney in 1968 by defeating fourth-ranked Duquesne for the championship. We had other big wins over St. John's, Oregon State (twice), Clemson, Georgetown, and Oklahoma in the 1970 NIT. Along with Pete, SEC players from that era drafted and playing successfully in the pros, beginning in 1970, included Issel and Larry Steele from the University of Kentucky, Tom Boerwinkle from Tennessee, Neal Walk from Florida, John Mengelt from Auburn, and Johnny Neumann at Mississippi. We had six-foot-nine Bill Newton and six-eight Dan Hester, who played in the ABA after leaving LSU.

Other top players from around the conference at the time were Rod Freeman, Tom Hagen, and Thorpe Weber at Vandy; Bob Croft at Tennessee; and Wendell Hudson at Alabama, to name a few. Also noteworthy was LSU's 1970–71 team, which finished third in the SEC—a year after Pete left. Four players from that team earned All-SEC honors, which was a tribute to our recruiting at the time.

⧉⧉⧉

While Press Maravich was fearless in scheduling nonconference opponents for his Tigers, there were times, as **BERNBROCK** *remembers, that he probably wishes he had scheduled some Division II patsy instead of, say, UCLA:*

I remember our first season together when our varsity faced a killer schedule and we were really outmanned most of the year. These were great kids, and we really admired their heart and dedication despite the fact our season was disappointing. One time we were in San Francisco and had just lost to Stanford in Palo Alto earlier that evening. We had UCLA the very next night at the Sports Arena in Los Angeles. Because these were back-to-back games over a twenty-four-hour period, we didn't want to focus on both teams, fearing that we would be looking ahead to the talented Bruins too much.

It was 11 P.M. when we returned to the Sir Frances Drake Hotel, and I loaded the film onto the projector so that Press, Jay (McCreary), and I could watch John Wooden's quick and aggressive team. I turned on the film and UCLA's pressing defense was so quick that it scared Press to no end. He asked me to please slow the film down, and I then had to give him the bad news—I already had the projector on slow motion! We went on to play a valiant game the next evening and almost upset UCLA, finally losing by just a few points.

⧉⧉⧉

MARAVICH, *on letting his hair down after he got to LSU:*

Another trademark (in addition to the floppy socks) I acquired was the mop-top hair style. It was a reflection of the maverick spirit I inherited from my brother, Ronnie. I enjoyed the longer hair styles the Beatles made popular in the 1960s and decided to wear my hair much longer than the normal short styles. At the time I could relate to a gifted athlete like Joe Namath who wanted sports to be unpredictable and fun. I believed a player should bring his own personality and excitement to his sport; otherwise, athletics would be filled with robots all marching to the same drummer.[2]

TOMMY HESS, *a guard, arrived at LSU a year after Maravich did, in part because his dad, James, also a basketball coach, had hit it off so well with Press Maravich:*

It was through my dad's being a high school basketball coach and coaching a blue-chip guy that he was able to establish relationships with a lot of college coaches. My dad and Press really hit it off. They were both good Christian people. Not only did they talk basketball, they talked that kind of stuff, although my dad was never a cusser or smoker, whereas Press liked to smoke cigars and say a few choice words. But he had a good heart. When Pete and Press were together at camp (in Pennsylvania), with Pete being a counselor by this time, when it was lights out at night, it was amazing to sit in a room and listen to them. I wish I could remember what was said. Pete used to make us laugh, such as when he and his dad would get on each other.

Pete would do the ballhandling drills and it'd just amaze the counselors. Spinning the ball on his finger, flipping it up and hitting it off his head into the basket, stuff like that. Shooting hook shots from halfcourt and guaranteeing that he would always make at least three out of ten—shooting like Meadowlark Lemon of the Globetrotters. We'd go out at night to get a sandwich and a beer or something like that at a diner, and Pete would always get steak and eggs, no matter where we'd go. Same thing at LSU. Instead of going to the Waffle House or McDonald's or Burger King, he'd always want to go to a diner where he would always get a T-bone steak and eggs.

⨯⨯⨯

*Another of Maravich's teammates at LSU was six-foot-eight forward **DANNY HESTER**, who arrived there before Pete's junior year as a junior-college transfer out of Oklahoma. Hester had been a JUCO All-American and had been invited to try out for the U.S. Olympic basketball team in 1968 (as had Pete). Hester was one of several LSU acquisitions who helped bolster the LSU program to the point where opponents had to be ready for another LSU player quite capable of scoring twenty or more points should they shut down Maravich:*

The first thing I remember about Pete is that when he was in one of the Olympic tryout games and he would go up for a lay-up, everyone would come over and try to block his shot, knocking into each other trying to get to it. That's the kind of attention he drew, and in each of our own minds, we were going to get to it. Then there were some boosters there from LSU, and my junior-college coach had coached for one of these guys and introduced me to him, and that's how things got rolling as far as my visitation to LSU among other places. When I was there for the weekend visit, we all scrimmaged, then went out for a few beers. Out of all the places I visited, that was the place where I needed to go, also in part because of all the national attention that he was getting. Press, his father, said, "If you come here and get rebounds, I'll guarantee you a pro tryout." So those kinds of things all fell together.

One thing really noticeable to me there was that the whole conference was pretty racially segregated. I came from a junior-college team on which ten or eleven of the fifteen guys were black. Plus I grew up in Illinois, so I was used to playing with black guys. I didn't realize that there was one black guy in the whole conference when I got there in 1968—Perry Wallace, who played at Vanderbilt. The whole league was white. It was unbelievable. I had conversations with both Pete and Press about it, and Press said, "We try to recruit black kids, but they can't go to parties other people go to and can't socialize." That's one of the main reasons why you didn't see any black players in the league back then. There weren't options for other races to play—just one of those facts of being in the sixties.

⋙⋘

Even though he wasn't an LSU basketball player, **Danny Young**'s *work in sports information drew him close to the team and their coaches, and in essence he became a part of the team, or at least its camaraderie, and that vantage point gave him a chance to see firsthand some of the wild side of Pete Maravich:*

Pete wasn't a hell-raiser when he first got here, but once he got settled into college life and started having some success, he started being pretty wild. There were some things that I saw working in the position I was in—some things on road trips. He'd go out on the road, drink, womanize, the whole nine yards, things you expect kids to do, but I'm sure there were some things I didn't even come close to knowing about.

I can't say I was extremely close to Pete. I was closer to Press than I was to Pete. As a young man, I matured early in life. When I worked for the athletic department, I was actually a junior or senior and then a grad student. I had this maturity level where I was pretty much accepted by the coaches, and I was kind of a step above the players from the standpoint of camaraderie, so they looked at me as kind of another coach or a Bud Johnson.

I had a strong relationship with one of the players, trying to straighten him out—Danny Hester—he always had trouble with Pete's getting the limelight and he wanted some of that. I spent a lot of time working with him trying to get him to realize the importance of playing with Pete. He was six-eight, a good rebounder, but he wanted to score. He had some good games scoring. I was probably closer to Danny than all of the players who played with Pete. He was very vocal about how Pete wouldn't give him the ball. And then he'd play beautifully one night and score and Pete would pass to him and he would pass to Pete, and then he'd have an off game and he would get mad again.

⊱∾⊰

Even if Maravich was a big man on campus, he didn't act like a big shot on campus. As fellow student and future newspaperman **JOE MACALUSO** *remembers it, Maravich was quite accessible on campus:*

Everybody on campus knew him. And unlike today where you see players driving around in really nice cars, he drove around in a Volkswagen, and everyone knew his Volkswagen. He didn't care a lot for school, but he went to class. He was a typical young guy who had the future all mapped out for him. I was in accounting at LSU, and two of the guards who played with him—Jeff Tribbett and Rich Hickman—took a lot of classes with me and we talked constantly about it. They knew where they were going. They were going into the business world somewhere. One (Hickman) is a successful businessman today and the other a CPA (Tribbett).

Pete was a playboy kind of guy. Back then, LSU was steeped in the past. This was in the late sixties and the restriction was no alcohol within a mile of campus. So Pete was always at places around town, and the drinking age was eighteen, so it wasn't too hard to drink once you got a mile away from campus. That little VW Beetle would turn up at several places a night.

I think he had the same girlfriend all through college—a college-sweetheart kind of thing. Everybody knew Pete Maravich. Back then, LSU had about twenty thousand students. He walked to class like everyone else did. He was very visible and everyone knew him. Floppy hair. Dressed like a lot of other people, but a skinny six-foot-five guy. People would pass right by him on the quadrangle. He was that kind of guy—he fit in. He lived at the jock dorm and ate at the training table like everyone else. His dad took special pains to make sure he was like one of the people.

✖

Maravich apparently felt quite comfortable in his familiar VW Beetle, as one interview subject for this book pointed out with a chuckle, although he didn't want to be identified with this story:

He never really had any run-ins with police, although one time the story was that the police found him asleep on the side of the interstate when it was being built. It was something like three o'clock in the morning. He had pulled up alongside the road and was sleeping, although he wasn't violating any laws as far as we know. You couldn't get him for vagrancy because, heck, this was a guy getting ready to make a gazillion dollars within a few months. So I guess they called the pop, got the right guy's number, and took him home.

✖

It was easy to criticize Maravich as being a one-dimensional player—an offensive genius and scoring machine who (supposedly) couldn't play a lick of defense, but as former LSU sports information director **BUD JOHNSON** *explains, don't rush to any false conclusions:*

Pete was always known as a scorer, but I have a vivid memory of him as a defensive player. I guess he was a senior at LSU and hurt his knee badly against somebody. About a week to ten days later we had a conference game with Mississippi State. And this was in the days of the four corners. So he got the mother of all tape-up jobs. He was taped from mid-thigh to mid-calf. I had never seen such an extensive taping job in all my life. It was done to immobilize that knee as much as possible.

State opens the game in the four corners, and they had this little point guard running the ball on the delay game, keeping the ball away from LSU and trying to get a good shot and hopefully win a slowdown game. There really was only one athlete on the LSU team that could guard this little guy and it was Pete. So Pete got on him and those two were playing man-to-man while everyone else played four corners. And gradually Pete wore him down. He had those long arms and he could slap the ball and reach in and knock the ball loose, and he stayed with this kid, who was pretty quick. He did a nose-to-nose defensive job on him, turned the game around, and LSU won the ball game. I remember coach Jay McCreary saying, "Well, Pete, you let the cat out of the bag—you can play defense." He was focused. He was competitive and he wanted to win that game, and this was his responsibility. No one else was going to take that point guard.

This was also in a day when most people in the SEC didn't know what an assist was. You'd go to some place like Alabama and see the stat crew, and they're all students and they're all cheering for Alabama. So are they recording assists correctly? Assists had to be defined by the conference office when I was in the league, unbelievably, for the SID. I'm not demeaning the SIDs—there were some really good ones, some better than me. But basketball was just not that big in the SEC at that time. You would have two sellouts in your season—Kentucky and Pete. All around the league, everywhere, same case. I saw a guy make a flying tackle of Pete at

Maravich goes airborne for two more of his 3,667 career points at LSU, a scoring mark that encompassed only three seasons and which still stands.

Ole Miss. No flagrant foul. In high school, I had seen guys thrown out for that.

All I can explain to you is that basketball came to the Southeastern Conference late. Let me give a good example. In late August, early September one year, the SEC had something called the Skywriters. They chartered a plane and would get all the guys (writers) on the plane and they would go from Vanderbilt to Ole Miss to Starkville to Tuscaloosa, to Auburn, and spend a day on the campus. Interview the coach, interview a star player, and then move on. This is how they got all their preseason material on every team in the league.

While this was going on, two guys came to me: the UPI sports editor from Atlanta and a writer from one of the Florida papers. They said to me early on, "Look, while we're in Baton Rouge, we want to get a one-on-one with Pete Maravich." So they get their exclusive with Pete. I delivered Pete to them in a place where they would not be seen by the rest of the group. Few days later, the story runs on the wire, the one generated by the UPI guy, and the Baton Rouge sports editor sees me at football practice and asks, "Have they started basketball practice already?" Basketball was not topical there except in basketball season. Here was an internationally known athlete that was considered news by somebody else year-round, yet in Baton Rouge, uh-uh, you're not news until your season starts.

By and large, the local papers didn't cover LSU out of town in those days, even with Maravich, which really told you that the SEC was really a basketball backwater at that time. I knew that and had a difficult time accepting that. Heck, I paid my own way to go to the NCAA Tournament in Louisville because I knew we had a national commodity. I went to the basketball writers breakfast there, saw Mitch Chortkoff from the *L.A. Times*, Billy Reed from Louisville, and a lot of guys. I buttonholed them and told them this guy was for real and he's worthy of preseason all-America's. At that point, the only other preseason all-America sophomore

I had heard of was Lew Alcindor. Well, Pete Maravich was a preseason all-America even before he had scored a varsity point, and that was based on what he had done as a freshman. Writers in Louisville and Los Angeles knew something that the writers in Louisiana didn't know. Like, what's wrong with this picture?

The only thing harder than being a member of the media and trying to get a one-on-one interview with Maravich was being a student at LSU and trying to get into one of the Tigers' games, as then-LSU student **JOE MACALUSO** *recalls. For that matter, road games weren't much easier for students from the opposing school:*

Back then, if LSU was playing, a lot of students would cut class to stand in line and get a seat. There were maybe eighteen hundred student seats in the Cowbarn. It wasn't like now where everyone gets a ticket. Back then, when they filled it up, that was it. If they had room for 1,820 and you were number 1,821, you didn't get in. There were times like that Kentucky game in 1970, Pete's last game against them, which was on a Saturday afternoon, that the line started on Friday morning.

I have a friend, a charter boat skipper who went to Mississippi State; I would drive down to the coast and go fishing. And we were talking once, and he was at Mississippi State in the late sixties, and I asked him if he went to see Pete Maravich play, and he said, "Yeah, we went all the time." He said he had an afternoon chemistry class and he cut it and his professor saw him. It was the same deal at Mississippi State. They had only a certain number of student seats and if you didn't get in line by 1:00 or 1:30 in the afternoon, you didn't get to see him play. It was a real phenomenon to go see him play. Even games at Kentucky. It happened everywhere he went. I remember going down to

Tulane when Maravich was a junior and Tulane was still playing in the bandbox that only seated something like forty-seven hundred people. People were lined up, and they never sold out at Tulane. That day we left school at 2:30 to get down there at 4:30 for a 7:30 game.

❧

Pete Maravich's freshman season at LSU wasn't an overnight success in terms of audience appeal, but it didn't take long for him (and his teammates, of course) to turn things around, as teammate **RANDY LAMONT** *remembers:*

We had a chance to rebuild the program at LSU. It was not a basketball powerhouse by any means and didn't have much of a following. But I think Baton Rouge gets behind any winning team. At the very first freshman game, there were maybe fifteen to twenty people in the stands and by the third game, they were filling seats at the Cow Palace and then leaving for the varsity game. Once we turned sophomore and started playing varsity, it was packed and we really had the chance to improve the basketball situation in Baton Rouge, which Pete really did. I give him credit for doing everything to get basketball at LSU back on track.

I had never heard of Pete before I came to LSU, but in our first practice we were getting hit in the head and the stomach with perfect passes. And we were trying to figure out where they came from. And how he did it! I mean, it was amazing. You knew something was getting ready to happen. In high school everything was a straight chest pass or bounce pass, and he was passing them behind his back, between his legs, and over his shoulders. We were probably black and blue getting hit with passes that were right there and which we just weren't ready for.

It started out being just a regular offense. Just screen and pick and rolls. As the season developed, it became more and more screens to allow Pete to shoot because he was such a great shooter. Lots of ballhandling and agility drills. As the season went along, especially after we went to the varsity, teams would start throwing all kinds of defenses at us. The first time we played a team Pete might score fifty or sixty points, so that the next time we played them they would have a different defense to try and prevent that. We had to keep adjusting our offense to try to get him or someone else open to take a shot. It seemed we might play someone the first time using a box and one on us, with four men around the lane and one man going to man to man on Pete, and by the end of the time it was the other way around, with four men on Pete and one guy on the rest of us.

The team chemistry was never much of a problem. Talked quite a bit about basketball and practice a lot even if it wasn't an organized basketball. Played a lot of pickup games. Pete loved to have a good time. We went out to movies and stuff. As a freshman, they didn't have the dorms completely finished. They were building new football players' dorms, and we had to stay in what they called Pleasant Hall for about six or eight weeks. Then the football players moved out of their old rooms into the new dorms and we moved into their old rooms in Broussard Hall. Pete was about the only one here when we were freshmen who had a car—a Volkswagen. It was hysterical seeing five or six of us climb into this little Volkswagen and venture off to the movies or wherever we were going. It looked like that old TV commercial with Wilt Chamberlain climbing out of that car. He was kind of the designated driver and he took us all over the place.

Then as sophomores, a few of us others got cars and that helped solve the crunch in his car. Anywhere we went, he was usually driving. There were three movie theaters downtown, and they aren't there now. The Paramount, the Hart, and the Gordon. All have been torn down. I remember there was one movie that we watched on TV, and it was a real scary movie, and Pete was one of these guys who loved to play practical jokes. After we saw this movie, which scared the heck out of us, for two weeks, every time you'd walk around a corner, Pete would jump out and go, "Boo!" and we'd jump about a foot into the air. It got old.

⋙⋘

Every now and then, especially during the summer, Maravich would venture off campus to find a quality pickup basketball game, and he usually didn't have to go far. According to longtime Baton Rouge resident **DONALD SPENCER**, *Maravich would often show up at a paved court near McKinley High School to play pickup games on pavement against black players from the city, and it was there that he squared off against some of his toughest opponents in the South:*

I never really met him. I was always off to the side because I was too small to be playing with those guys. I just stayed back swinging on a swing or standing on the sidelines, watching the games. It was almost better to watch than to play when it came to sandlot basketball. This was just outside the gates to LSU—walking distance. Coach Carl Stewart, at McKinley at that time, always had a dynamic player, and he was the type of person that would take them wherever they wanted to go. It was unusual for someone like Pete Maravich to be white and not from that area but playing in those games. Sandlot basketball was better than high school basketball at that time. It was like an all-star game.

There was no coaching. One thing I remember is that Pete always looked like he was sick. But he would sit on the side and spin the ball on his finger. He had to wait to get into those games. He stood out because he was white. But when he did get in there to play, you had him and black guys like Fred Hilton, Marvin Turner, and John Chaney—you're looking at the most talented players in the state of Louisiana right there. Hilton played for Grambling. All-SWAC. He and Pistol Pete are the only two people I ever saw who took two steps across the halfcourt line and let it go—a jump shot, and they had no three-point rule in effect then. It was two points for every shot you made. Marvin Turner and Pete Maravich are the only people I ever saw who could take the ball from behind their back and go with it between the legs and make a crip without walking. All that Harlem Globetrotter stuff they would be doing—this was legitimate because you had to be doing this in a game.

⬥

As word of Maravich's exploits spread throughout the South, basketball started rivaling football for the people's attention, as **New** Orleans Times-Picayune *sportswriter* **MARTY MULE** *explains:*

I was at LSU the same time as Pete, so I saw almost every home game and some away games. I also covered the Jazz when they were in New Orleans, so other than his father, I probably saw more of Pete Maravich's games than anybody else. I didn't see the freshman year, but I knew how the fans would leave after the freshman game. It was Press's first season and the varsity's record was something like 3-23. The next year they were 14-12, which although by itself wouldn't open many eyes, it was like a 900 percent increase from what they were the year before.

Pete made basketball in the South. Across the South, a lot of kids that would have been halfbacks or tight ends were now becoming guards and forwards. As far as I'm concerned, he popularized what was an off-season between football and spring football in the South. Clyde Bolton in Birmingham recently wrote a column in which he asked C. M. Newton, who has spent thirty or forty years in the SEC, that if he had to pick one basketball player from the SEC who would it be. C. M. instantly said Pistol Pete, and the reason was because of the intensity and the passion with which he played the game, and the fact that he did things in basketball that hadn't been seen before and haven't been seen since. And I believe that. Pete was the greatest ballhandler ever. People talk a lot about the shooting, but to me the greatness of Pete Maravich was his ballhandling. He was a great shooter, sure, but you had to see his ballhandling to believe it.

In Pete's last season at LSU, their regular-season record was something like 20-8 and they finished second in the SEC. It came down to LSU's last home game against Kentucky for the SEC title, and in that game Pete and Dan Issel had a shootout. Pete had something like 52 and Issel something like 48. Kentucky beat them and LSU ended up going to the NIT and Kentucky to the NCAAs, but in today's world LSU would also have been in the NCAAs.

⚜

MARAVICH, *after his freshman season at LSU, on going to California and seeing a buddy step forward at a Campus Crusade for Christ altar call to receive Jesus Christ as his personal Savior:*

When I saw my friend start to stand, I grabbed him . . . I couldn't believe my ears. I thought, how could anyone fall for something so stupid. I could see it now—two thousand miles back home in the car with a Jesus freak! As he walked toward the counselors, I played it cool and bowed my head, not wanting to draw any attention to myself. I had played this game before in my parents' church, and I knew the invitation would end soon and I could breathe easier once again.[3]

⚜

MULE, *the* Times-Picayune *sportswriter who had some overlap time at LSU with Maravich, doesn't remember Maravich as having a constantly sunny disposition:*

I rubbed shoulders with him, but I was more friends with his dad than with him. Pete was a little standoffish and could be a little sullen. But his dad was a gregarious, really funny guy who I think is overlooked a lot in basketball lore. He was an offensive innovator and he was really a good offensive coach.

I saw Pete a lot around school and saw him even more when he was with the Jazz. We had a relationship of sorts, not a friendship really, but it was cordial and we spent some time with each other. He was a much more complete ballplayer as a pro than he had been as a collegian. A lot of people don't see the difference, but if you look at Pete as a collegian, you see a skinny kid who could do a lot with the ball, but as a pro he was pretty filled out, having worked out with weights and so forth.

He always said, but he was wrong, that there was nothing he did in the pros that he couldn't do in high school. For one thing he could dunk in the pros and he couldn't do that in college or high school, and he could do that because he was a much bigger, stronger guy. He was a little stand-offish until the day he died. He was a little suspicious of people—he had been burned in the press a few times. He was never the life of the party type of guy, at least with the general public.

⚇

*As high as Maravich's star rose at LSU, an occasional campus incidence of humility would keep his head out of the clouds, as **MULE** explains:*

The students worshiped him, but it wasn't like he couldn't walk around campus. He used to tool around in a little Volkswagen. The story goes that he parked on a hill on campus near the journalism school with the football stadium at the bottom of a hill, where the basketball offices were. Pete parks his car at the top of the hill and he's got shades on, and he sees this little coed running down the street with books under her arm on her way to class, and he leans back against his Volkswagen with his arms folded as she goes by and says,

"Hello, Paula." And she looks up and goes, "Oh, hi. Hi. Do I know you?" He kind of pulls the glasses back and says, "I'm Pete Maravich." And she goes, "Aren't you a track star or something?" He might have been a big man on campus, but it wasn't universal.

※※※

Playing on the same team with Maravich, at LSU at least, oftentimes meant being "subjected" to the same kind of drills that Pistol Pete had been practicing every day for the last fifteen years, as attested to by **RALPH JUKKOLA:**

When Pete first came here, we had heard how great he was. When you first saw the kid, it was like, "Good God, this guy can't be any good because he was like six-five and about 155 pounds. Nobody really respected him much until you saw him play, but then you saw what he could do with the ball. In the long run, it made all of us a little bit better ballplayers. Press made us go through some of these drills, ballhandling drills, that Pete probably could have done blindfolded. It got to be a thing where we all tried different things Pete was doing, and it helped us all. Some people may not admit that. I came from a high school where if you threw a pass behind your back, you had better make sure it got to the person you were throwing it to or you'd be over on the pine with the coach. His style of basketball was something that you otherwise saw only with the Globetrotters. It was outstanding to play with.

　　If you got open, he would probably get you the ball. He liked to pass more than he liked to shoot, contrary to what a lot of people think, knowing that he averaged forty-four points a game. If he hadn't been forced to shoot so much of the time, he would have had even more assists. He made a lot of great passes, but when you're scoring forty-four points a game, it doesn't leave you a whole lot of room in the statistics to get a lot more assists, or even chances at assists. We went from 3-20 to 14-12 and then 13-13. We really picked it up the next year (1969–70). My senior year, we started off real well, but then we got into the conference and never jelled. We went totally berserk, and that was around the time that Press said that Pete needed to be shooting forty times a game. Most of the guys who were complaining were the guys who weren't playing anyway.

❧

Maravich had a deep bag of basketball tricks that he never hesitated to pull out, and if you watched him closely, you could see that he had almost as many different facial expressions that he exhibited in the heat of battle, as touched on by former Sports Illustrated *basketball guru and writer* **CURRY KIRKPATRICK:**

From a distance, Maravich on the court often gives an impression of complete nonchalance. But close up, his face reveals him for the player that he is. His expressions are forever contorted and wrenched into horrible forms of pain, cruelty, and even torture. He bares his teeth a lot, and his tongue hangs out of the corner of his mouth when he is acting really tough. Sometimes he takes on the look of a man being pumped full of bullets. . . . Maravich's conversation is almost always ingenuous. His direct, open style and his easygoing, unaffected nature are perhaps the major factors responsible for the close camaraderie existing between the star and his supporting players.[4]

❧

An argument could be made that SEC basketball hovered near mediocrity before Maravich came along to rescue the league, but that's forgetting the fact that perennial powerhouse Kentucky belonged to the SEC and had cranked out a number of outstanding players over the years, to include a foursome of Dan Issel, Mike Pratt, Larry Steele, and Mike Casey that a

number of times had the opportunity to go up against
Maravich and the Tigers. But SEC wasn't really a one-
team league (Kentucky), and its talent pool that year
went well beyond one man (Maravich), as Auburn star
guard **JOHN MENGELT** *recalls:*

Not only did you have Issel, Steele, and Pratt at Kentucky,
but we also had players like Neal Walk at Florida and
Tommy Hagen at Vanderbilt. It was a stronger conference
than people knew. Kentucky was obviously the strongest,
but Tennessee, Vandy, and Florida were good. Bama had a
couple of good years, but couldn't get over the hump. LSU
finished a little back all the time, but they had "the show" so
they got a lot of publicity. We had some really good players
there, but there just wasn't any interest or publicity down
South. All we had back then was Street and Smith's. We'd
run out and buy it as soon as it came out so we could read
what was going on in college basketball and to see our name.
SI didn't give a crap.

The presence of Maravich and Issel helped me get some
notoriety—it rubbed off. It didn't hurt when I scored forty-
five points up at Kentucky and there were (NBA) scouts in
the stands there watching those guys. Back in those days,
scouting was so unsophisticated, they could miss you. Guys
would have to fly and then drive to get to Auburn, Alabama,
and who the heck wants to do that? They'd rather stay in
Atlanta or someplace they could get out. Nowadays, you've
got satellite dishes and all that stuff and you can't hide anybody, not even someone playing NAIA.

Nobody talked to me. Nobody worked me out. Nobody
knew how tall I was except what they read in the game program before they drafted me, and I was the seventeenth
player drafted. There were seventeen teams and two of them
didn't have draft choices, so I was Cincinnati's second
choice. They chose Kenny Durrett out of LaSalle—he tore
his ACL even before they knew what it was. He was better
than Dr. J. Fourth game of his second year got hurt again.

They paid him $900,000 for five years and that was huge back then.

❧

Getting back to Maravich as a freshman, and this at a time when freshmen were ineligible to play varsity ball, it was Bernbrock's task to groom these young Tigers to be ready to graduate to Press Maravich's varsity. It was a task performed almost to perfection, as Bernbrock's freshmen performed admirably, winning their first seventeen games before losing the finale by one point at Tennessee. BERNBROCK remembers it as an exciting season punctuated by the opportunity to spend a year coaching the Pistol:

Coaching Pete his freshman year was quite an experience. Pete was a "gamer" to the nth degree. Press and I used to differentiate among players in recruiting, especially the guys with "terminal potential," or "7:30 shooters," as we called them. You had to be able to identify the players who turned it on at eight o'clock when the game started in front of fifteen thousand people, and Pete was one of those!

We dominated our schedule, winning seventeen in a row, only to lose the last game by a point at the buzzer at Tennessee. Pete missed the final free throw in the game, and he felt so bad about it that he walked back to the hotel on his own so as to burn off the frustration. He hated to lose. We played a three-guard offense with Pete in the middle and Jeff Tribbett and Rich Hickman on the wings, and Randy Lamont and Drew Corley in a double post. That offense was perfect for Pete's freewheeling, give-and-go style of basketball.

From early on in our season the freshman games were sellouts. Home and away, thousands of people flocked to see Pete and our team play. It was exciting basketball, and the kids averaged close to a hundred points a game. Our favorite play was what we called "the special" where we went cross-directional with the guards and brought Pete under the basket and back out behind a double screen for a jump shot. We had plenty of options depending on the defense, but Pete had to have hit 90 percent of his shots off that play throughout the season. Maravich was a deadly long-range shooter, and that was back when there was no three-point shot. You can only imagine how many career points he would have scored had there been a three-point basket in that era.

I did all of the coaching of the freshman team that season. Press and I shared the same basketball philosophy, and in preparing the kids for varsity play, we naturally had identical goals and objectives. It's like any team or successful company where you have a culture, system, or prescribed way of operating. Press's influence on his son began almost at birth, so the work ethic, the basketball knowledge, etc., had been instilled by Press from Pete's earliest years. When he was in grade school, he used to take a basketball to the movies and sit on the aisle, dribbling in the dark to develop fingertip control. All of this Maravich magic started very early in Pete's childhood years. It's a great story and a very special and unique bond between father and son.

Pete was as genuine as they come, and he was born to play basketball. He also had a humorous side to him, even in pressure situations. Every once in a while after throwing a fancy pass or faking someone out big time, he'd look over at the coaches and wink as if to say, "That one's for you, Dad." What I remember most about him is how right before we would break the huddle following the playing of the national anthem, his eyes would look up at the scoreboard. Showtime was about to begin!

Hess, like Maravich, was born in Pennsylvania and later attended the Campbell College summer camp where he learned basketball alongside Pete, but the main selling point in getting **HESS** *to commit to LSU and not one of the number of Pennsylvania or other eastern* *schools that pursued him was actually a football game—a game at the Swamp:*

When I went down to visit LSU my senior year in high school, it was during football season, and I was down there with two other guys. We went to Tiger Stadium with seventy-something thousand people and the tigers in the cages and cheerleaders sitting on the cages, and they put microphones on the cages and made the tigers growl and roar. I also had a beautiful sorority girl as a date, and that game just excited the heck out of me. I wasn't even thinking Pistol Pete then.

That's what brought me to LSU, and of course once I got there I already knew Pistol Pete, who had gotten there a year ahead of me. I was able to be a part of college basketball history. I'm the only athlete to break a Pistol Pete record, although some have probably been broken since. I broke Pete's freshman assists record. We had a good team—eight scholarship players on that team. In practice, I had to guard him. I was able to stay with him for the most part, but he was able to shoot over me a lot because he was six-five and I was five-ten. But he never tried to show off or make me or others look bad. He was like one of the guys—a lot of fun to be around. Because he was a superstar, we were able to see what it's like to be stampeded by young kids and overanxious daddies, even girls and stuff like that, on an up-and-up level. There was a big following, but it was something that he had earned. This was a guy scoring over forty points a game without a three-point line.

There were three senior guards and a sophomore guard, me. Press asked me if I wanted to redshirt, which would have been the smart move because I didn't play much. I played in seventeen of the thirty-two games, usually just to mop up. But I had an opportunity to travel with the team and be privy to some exciting moments—Pete's great game-ending hook shot at Georgia, playing at UCLA when the Bruins had Henry Bibby, Curtis Rowe, Sidney Wicks, John

Vallely and, of course, John Wooden. Pistol had a bunch of turnovers in the first half. That was the only time I saw Pistol sort of struggle a little bit because most challenges he met easily. But that was a tough loss—the worst beating we ever had. They trashed the heck out of it. That's when I met Mike Connors, the guy from Mannix. I met him and a few other famous people, and that's all because of Pistol Pete. We went to Hawaii and spent ten beautiful days there, and that's probably going to be the only time in my life that I'll get to Hawaii.

There were a lot of things Pete was able to do on the floor that were just miraculous. I can remember when we were playing St. John's. I believe it was in the semifinals of the Rainbow Classic in Hawaii, and St. John's had just scored in a halfcourt set. Somebody took the ball out and everyone was making the transition back. The guy guarding Pistol was right at the foul line. One of the LSU players, Apple Sanders I think, threw the ball into Pistol, who had his back to the defender. Pete received the basketball, and as he turned, and it was like ten thousand people there watching this and there's no way he could have known that this guy had just come up on him out of nowhere, so to speak. As he turned, Pete sensed that the guy was there, and he was in a great defensive position. In one fluid movement, Pete turned, put the ball through the guy's legs, went around him, and continued his dribble down the court. I know that sounds so elementary and simple, but you would have just had to see it. It was so fantastic just having the awareness to know that somebody was there.

⊷⊶

The Maravich years at LSU were some of the best years in LSU sports history, as his time in Baton Rouge overlapped the college careers of football stars there such as defensive back **TOMMY CASANOVA** *and quarterback Bert Jones. Not only was there a sense of mutual admiration between the LSU football and* *basketball players, but for Casanova, now an ophthalmologist in Crowley, Louisiana, the Pistol Pete era at LSU found him to be one of Pete's biggest fans in the stands for every home basketball game:*

I knew him moderately well. He was a couple years older than me. A real quiet guy. I knew some of the younger basketball players that were my same year. I never missed a game. When they were in town playing, I was there. Pete was just unbelievable on the basketball court. I had played high school basketball and was the type of player who would get the rebound and pass the ball to somebody else. Honest to God, I'm sure Michael Jordan is the greatest basketball player in the world, but Pete Maravich could do things with a basketball that I'm sure Michael Jordan has never even thought of. Pete didn't have the athletic ability Michael Jordan has—nobody does—but as far as handling a basketball, knowing where people were open on the court, and overall sense of basketball, I'd match Pete Maravich up against anybody.

It got to be almost humorous. Pete never took an easy shot. If he had an open ten-footer, he would rather drive to the bucket and try to draw a foul and get three points. He seldom took an open shot because he was looking for an advantage every time. I'm sure his scoring record will never be approached, but if they had had the three-point shot when Pete was in college, goodness knows what his scoring average would have been because then he would have taken all those open shots from the outside instead of driving and hoping to get fouled for a three-point play.

One night, and I don't remember who we were playing, he came down the left-hand side of the court, unguarded, near the sideline, took one step over halfcourt, stopped, and with two hands he just let it go. It was nothing but net, and the place went absolutely crazy. I mean, it was not a basketball play, and his dad just sat there like it was no big deal, and any other coach would have had a seizure. Pete gets the ball again next time and goes right to the same spot and lets it fly. Nothing but net. Third time he comes down and goes to the same place and lets it go, and this time the ball rattles inside the rim—buh-buh-buh-buh-buh-buh—before it bounces out. He didn't do it anymore after that, but he was going to keep shooting that shot until he missed. And that's what you expected from him. Certainly, he was a team player, but he didn't have the support he needed to win a Southeastern Conference championship. Basketball was not LSU's strength back in those days.

⁙

The addition of Hester from the junior-college ranks before the 1968–69 season gave the Tigers a strong inside scoring threat to complement Maravich's outside and penetrating moves, but it didn't change the fact that LSU's basketball world revolved around Maravich. **HESTER,** *now a regional sales manager for Ciba Vision Corp., a contact-lens company, later played briefly in the pros with Denver and Kentucky:*

Most of our plays were structured around Pete. A lot of pick and rolls. That was pretty much it—set some picks out there, and let Pete move around and do what he can do, and if you're open he'll hit you and if not, he's going to take the shot. It's hard to describe the capability he had to get open as often as he did. Most people don't have that quickness or that ability to find the open spot. We had three big guys— myself, Bill "Fig" Newton, and Apple Sanders—and we'd get a lot of offensive rebounds—I know we were in the top ten of the league in rebounding both our junior and senior years. We'd set the picks for Pete and get ready to get the rebounds, if necessary.

The pros to this arrangement started with the fact you got a lot of attention. We had a full house everywhere we went. We set an attendance record for UCLA at Pauley Pavilion, and this was even after the Lew Alcindor years.

Pete had that kind of impact. We had some national TV games, although TV was nothing like it is today. To have national TV exposure was something very rare, and we had something like five or six games on television that last year. It was fun, not only at games but also at practices. One of the negatives, you could say, was that in some of the games the guy would not be hitting, but he would continue to shoot. But that was part of the whole deal, too.

We had a commonality there in that I think I was a pretty good ballplayer and he saw and respected that. We'd go out sometimes on the road on the night before a game and maybe shoot some pool, sometimes just the two of us. But I don't know if anybody really got close enough to him to be able to say, "Hey, he's my main bud." I can recall times we would go over to their house and his mom would come out from the back of the house raging about whatever was going on at the time, and we would just get out of there. But you never saw that publicly and it never was discussed. I didn't see that as an issue with him, although it might have been an underlying issue that just didn't come out.

One of the most incredible things with him I saw was a game we played against Alabama on the road. He sprained an ankle, giving him two sprained ankles, and he still got sixty-nine points. He played with a lot of pain and already had bad knees. Another interesting experience, and this was at a time when black people could not go to the white bars, was when we had been out running around a little bit; after a while we went over to north Baton Rouge where the black bars are. We just went into one of them, and Pete just started dribbling the basketball around. Up on the tables, around the chairs, and these people were just going wild. They knew who he was, and the place was just going nuts. He could do that. That was a fun night.

Our favorite hangout was Southdowns. It was like the cool place to go. A lot of football and basketball players went there. The younger-type boosters would be there, hanging out. Lots of chicks, too. Naturally, there were girls hanging out near Pete, and you're going to have that with a guy like that. But to be honest with the guy, he and Jackie were together throughout college and he didn't play around too much. He was a shy kid. These girls would come on to him and he was real shy—really shied away from them. We—the other guys—got the overages. We got the spillover.

For most of his first three years at LSU, Maravich palled around with his teammates, such as **RALPH JUKKOLA,** *although it is generally agreed that Maravich became somewhat more aloof and standoffish as a senior being subjected to intense glare from the media. All things considered, though, Maravich was a team player on and off the court, as Jukkola fondly remembers:*

I didn't run with him all the time. He stuck more with the guys he came to LSU with, even though he was older than them. Pete was about a week younger than me. As a team, we pretty much went places together, and all in all we got along well. There wasn't a lot of hostility or anything like that. Pete and I double-dated a few times, that kind of stuff. He was a good guy, fun to be around. He got into a little trouble a few times, stuff that's been documented. When he got away and had a beer or two, that's when he was blowing off some pressure. Over time he probably got a little less inhibited because these were times there weren't reporters around or someone around asking all these questions, where people don't really care if you're Pistol Pete or Ralph Jukkola or whatever. Baton Rouge at the time was a good little place, but not what you would call a rip-roaring place. It's a big country town more than it's a small big town—more of a laid-back atmosphere. We are the capital of the state, but we aren't huge. You can get from one end of town to the other in a reasonable amount of time.

Some of the guys belonged to fraternities, and if they had a big party, the rest of us would usually get invited. With Pete there, we got a lot more notoriety—more people knew us. When I first came down here, I went to a few high school basketball games with some of the guys. I came back one time after seeing a couple of games and went to one of the coaches and said, "Coach, they don't have any black high school basketball players down here? All we saw were white players." Come to find out, which astonished me at the time, the blacks had their own league. I came from Ohio and that was a culture shock to me. The blacks' standard of ball was a little better and then they started desegregation and things got a little better, and they got to where basketball coaches were coaching basketball instead of an assistant football coach coaching the basketball team. There were two sports down here—football and spring football.

Pete helped change all that. We used to tour preseason different places in the state and put on a little exhibition or scrimmage, and the stuff Pete did—he was so far ahead of his time what he did with a basketball—the interest in the state really picked up. By the time I got out of school, you could go around and see kids dribbling between their legs and going behind their backs. Before, you would be lucky to even see a kid pick up a basketball. A lot of people try to credit Dale Brown with bringing basketball to Louisiana, but my feeling is that the Maraviches got it started in Louisiana.

❦

*LSU had frat houses and **RICH HICKMAN** and Jeff Tribbett were among the players who pledged, and as good as the parties were there (Hickman was Kappa Sigma, for example), some of the best fun, as Hickman recalls, was off campus. Well off campus:*

We went to a lot of fraternity parties. I'm not so sure Pete ever joined a fraternity, although I know he was looking at

SAE with Jeff, but if he ever did pledge a frat, he was certainly a nonactive frat brother. I just wanted to meet some different people than what you would meet in the athletic dorm.

One summer some of us, including Pete, went to Fort Lauderdale for about three days. We had about five bucks cash between us, and Russ Bergman had an old Cadillac. His alternator was going out, and by the time we got back to Baton Rouge we didn't have any headlights left, and we thought we were about going to die before we got back to the dormitory. We checked back in with no lights on, and when he turned that car off, it didn't start again. We did what every other college kid did down there—lots of sun, chase women, and drink a little beer. Got burned to a crisp, and when we got back Press just chewed all over us. We were about blistered and he reamed us a new backside. There were also places out on the lake that we would go visit on weekends a lot of the time—barbecue and ride boats out on the lake. We pretty much did things together, whether it was going out to eat, going to a party, or going to the movies or the drive-in.

Out of all of LSU's SEC opponents, none were more successful in shutting down Maravich while beating the Tigers than Tennessee, which had seven-foot center **TOM BOERWINKLE** *down low in the middle helping to make life miserable for Maravich and crew. Boerwinkle had already been at Tennessee when Pete got to LSU:*

Kentucky was the dominant force in that era and then other colleges started to emerge. Tennessee was starting to become known more for basketball, but Kentucky and Adolph Rupp was still the target everyone shot at. Kentucky and Tennessee were the two best. But Florida had a good program, as did Vanderbilt. With LSU, it wasn't the program, it was that Pete Maravich was down there. Everybody was really interested to see what he could do. His persona had preceded him into the SEC—the floppy socks and shaggy hair. One thing you always heard about Pete playing for Press was that Pete really ran the program—he did whatever he wanted to do. Whether that was true or not, I don't know. It was always felt that Pete had a pretty free hand to do whatever he wanted to do as far as basketball went at LSU.

⊱⊰

*The way Auburn guard **JOHN MENGELT** saw it, the South's ongoing emergence in basketball was due in part to Yankee influence. A number of SEC schools were diligently pursuing Northern-spawned talent (Maravich was born in Pennsylvania, remember). Not only had LSU pulled Maravich in, they had gone out and successfully recruited the likes of guard Jeff Tribbett, who had been a high school teammate of Purdue superstar Rick Mount at Lebanon High School in Indiana. Said Mengelt:*

We played a different brand of basketball up North. Pete was already in that mold and changed the league from being one of "Let's walk the ball up the floor and see how good a defense we can play," to "Let's speed the thing up and make it a little bit of a show." One factor was in recruiting the caliber of the player and then the style of the player made it a little more enjoyable, at least from a fan's objective. But even then the league's newfound basketball success was kind of localized. We didn't have the national prominence. There was one game a week on TV, there was no *USA Today*, and you just didn't get a lot of publicity. Because of the way Pete played and who he was, and how flamboyant he was in what he did and how he drew some attention to the conference, if Pete Maravich were playing today, that's all you would probably hear about.

I came out of Indiana—a little town called Ellwood, about thirty miles outside Indianapolis. In high school I was

essentially a six-two, fairly slow, small forward, and none of
the Big Ten schools or other big schools were really interested in me. From my senior year in high school to freshman
year in college I got a lot stronger and a lot quicker and
worked very, very hard in the summers to change myself
into a guard, and that made a great deal of difference.

The thing you've got to remember is that basketball even
in the summer in Indiana was probably bigger than college
basketball in the middle of the season in the South. We
would draw four hundred or five hundred people a night in
the summer to watch games on outdoor courts matching
town against town. And that wasn't just high school kids.
You could play as long as you wanted to play and were able
to play, and we had some guys out there twenty-five or thirty
years old playing against seventeen- and eighteen-year-old
kids, so you could really improve your game.

I visited very few schools that had any real interest in
me, and I felt like Auburn was the right place to be, and I
guess I made the right choice. I grew up in a very modest
family and had five siblings and my father made very little
money, so my choice was whichever place would pay my
way through school. I did have a few choices because I did
also play football and baseball, but being from Indiana,
you're going to play basketball somewhere.

Recruiting wasn't a very sophisticated game yet. There
was very little filming of games and very little video, and if
you weren't a star, nobody came to see you. So I was one of
those guys who was only seventeen my freshman year in
college and matured a lot, got a lot stronger and quicker,
which allowed me to move back and play guard. A six-two
forward ain't going to do too much in college unless he can
really leap, and God didn't bless me that way, although I
could shoot.

※≫≫≫≫≫

*The Tennessee Vols pretty much had Maravich's
number, and it wasn't forty-four, as in forty-four points*

a game. The Vols won five of six games against a Maravich-led LSU team over three years, holding him to twenty-three points a game and allowing him to score at least thirty only once, and even then it was exactly thirty in Tennessee's one-point victory over the Tigers late in the 1969–70 season. **BOERWINKLE** *sheds some light on how this was accomplished:*

I can remember one situation and am not certain how it transpired; Pete had averaged something like forty-five points a game and he needed to score X number of points in the last two or three games to set some kind of scoring record. And we held him to about half that. Tennessee was extremely successful shutting him down, but it's been too many years to tell you exactly how we did it. Our main defense was a trapping type defense, and we had players that could really cover areas very well. One of our players was Tom Hendricks—we called him Spook—and he ran the base line. His responsibility was to cover corner to corner along the base line. That was very much a key to our defense. Bill Justus was a great ballplayer and Billy played on one of the wings and was a great trapping player. Billy Hann played out on the point, and Ronnie Whitby was there my junior year playing that other wing.

It was just a situation where I think we played our standard defense, although Billy (Hann) was the one given more the responsibility of staying with Pete all over the floor, and we were triple-teaming him in some instances. Second or third guy collapsing on him. In basketball when playing against a great player, whether it's a Pete Maravich, a Jerry West, a Walt Frazier, or a Nate Archibald, there are always two theories—Kareem another example—one, you let the superstar get his points and shut down everyone else, or two, make the other people beat you, not the star. Obviously against LSU, we took the approach to first shut Pete down, and if they were going to beat us they were going to have to beat us with their other people, and I don't think they were very successful in beating us. As great a player as Pete was, and he certainly was a magician with the basketball, when he played against Tennessee, I think we frustrated him and forced him into taking a lot of bad shots. I would venture to say that not only did he not score as many points against Tennessee, but he didn't get off as many quality shots.

I think everybody thought Pete was a good guy. Everyone knew he was a little cocky and had a little bit of a swagger to him, but what players thought about when they played Pete was that they didn't want to be embarrassed. Pete could embarrass you. He could embarrass you terribly. You were unable to predict where he was going to deliver the ball, how he was going to deliver it, whether between his legs, behind his back, over his head, maybe all around his back and over to the other side—he was just a creative passer.

✎

When it was Georgia's turn to play LSU, the onus of guarding Maravich usually fell on Bulldogs guard **HERB WHITE**, *who later would join Pete as a teammate with the NBA's Atlanta Hawks for one season. White compared the energetic, elusive Maravich to another great star who had gone by the moniker of Perpetual Motion:*

They talked about how (John) Havlicek was in great shape and could run you to death, but I always thought that Pete was tougher to keep up with. I never guarded Pete in the pros, although I guarded him in practice and in college, and he was in unbelievable condition, always moving. He had three or four big guys there at LSU, big gorillas, setting picks for him and you were constantly running into them, so it was really a nightmare. I guarded him every time we played them in college. There was no worse feeling in the world than going down to Baton Rouge on Saturday night and having to try to hold their hero under fifty points in front of ten or twelve thousand half-drunk Cajuns. It was an old place and it was wild.

I would try to play him as rough as I could, but it was almost impossible because you couldn't keep up with him. They had the screens going, and he had the green light to shoot any time he wanted to, so he didn't worry about missing shots or taking bad shots. Trying to guard a guy like that is almost impossible, especially if he doesn't care. There was a game at Athens my junior year and it came down to the last few minutes of the game. I had fouled out, which I did all the time when trying to guard Pete. I think I had held him to seventeen points in the first half, which is about as good as you could do. In the last couple minutes of the game with the ball and the lead, we froze the ball because there was no shot clock then and we got it down to something like twelve or fifteen seconds to go.

We had a little guard from West Virginia named Jerry Epling, who was all-SEC and a good player averaging seventeen or eighteen points a game. He was a good little shooter but not quite as good as he thought he was. He decided he was going to take a jump shot—he was always taking it personally that he was going to show Pete that he could shoot with him—and he took a jump shot from the top of the circle with twelve seconds left, when all we had to do was hang on to the ball that long and win the game. Anyway, he shoots and misses, they get the rebound and go down and score to tie the game up and it goes into overtime. Then goes into a second overtime and the place is just going crazy. The arena only held about ten or eleven thousand people and they had thirteen thousand–plus people in there. Whenever Pete came to town, the fire marshals would just hide out somewhere. It was just incredible. Just a madhouse.

They finally had the ball and the lead with about a minute and a half left in the second overtime, and they gave the ball to Pete. He was out there dribbling around and we were out there trying to catch him and either foul him or steal the ball, and we couldn't even do that. He went into this kind of Globetrotter routine, going between his legs and behind his back, and it was just incredible. Guys were falling down and couldn't catch up to him.

Finally, as the clock is running down, with about five seconds to go, he dribbled the ball right toward our bench at the far end of the floor, and then dribbled out toward halfcourt—and as he got to halfcourt he just turned around and threw up this hook shot from like forty or fifty feet and the buzzer went off as the ball was in the air, and he just knocked the bottom out of the basket—boom! It wasn't the winning basket because they already had the lead, but it was the exclamation point. Our fans came pouring out of the stands, and they had him up carrying him off the floor and it was a celebration down in that end, and it was our gym! That was the kind of excitement that he could generate. He drove people crazy. No one had ever seen anything like that.

⟨⟨⟨⟩⟩⟩

When Auburn played LSU, it was **JOHN MENGELT'S** *turn to spearhead the defense against Maravich, which was a role that Mengelt could appreciate because he was a prolific scorer as well:*

I was a year behind Pete. I remember getting to school, and we would play pickup games right away and hearing the myth about Pete and all about the floppy socks, and how people came to watch the freshman game at LSU and then the freshman game was all over and they would all leave. The first taste I got of him was my freshman year. Freshmen weren't eligible to play then. But in getting ready for the varsity game against LSU, the freshman guys would run the LSU offense for practice and I was anointed to be Pete Maravich. And I've got to tell you something: I can't believe what he would have to do and the energy that he would have to expend to get open with or without the ball. I was totally exhausted after trying to pretend being him. It helped me because I learned that I had to get myself into better condition if I wanted to be as good as him. My first playing exposure against him was as a sophomore—he had a fair game playing against us the first time—I'm sure he had thirty or thirty-five points (forty-six, actually), but I think we did a pretty good job on him here and at their place. I doubt there was ever anybody in college basketball who was a better scorer than he was.

⋘⋙

When it came time to play the real Maravich and not simply act like him, **Mengelt** *sometimes found the reality much more taxing than the pretending:*

I would beat him up, as much as the refs would let me. You weren't going to keep Pete from scoring—all you could do was make him take more shots than he usually took. Not to downgrade him, but his shooting percentage was never really good, so the trick was to force him to take as many bad shots as possible, because outside of him and Jeff Tribbett, they didn't have much of anybody else who could shoot. What you had to do to play Pete was to force him to, one, shoot from the outside, and two, try not to foul him. I would beg my teammates not to foul him because he would pick up eleven, twelve, or thirteen of those points on the free-throw line. I knew because I averaged about thirty and I would do the same—try to get fouled as much as I could. Sometimes you take it to the hoop even knowing that you probably couldn't make it, but you knew there was a good chance that you were going to get fouled.

I didn't try to foul him while he was shooting. I was smart enough to know when they were in the bonus and that kind of thing and to not foul him when he was shooting, because he was several inches taller than I was and really had a great knack of going to the basket and putting his body on people, and I think I learned a lot from that. Pete was very, very good at that and scored a lot of points at the free-throw line and made a lot of three-point plays. He had too much stamina and could handle the ball too well. If a guy can't handle the ball well, you can just take him out of the game by faceguarding him without the ball and get some help coming off picks. But when you got a guy who can do both—score and handle the ball—you're in trouble.

<hr />

*Getting back to Tennessee and its success in clamping down on Maravich, Vols guard **BILL JUSTUS** said it was characteristic of Tennessee in those days to win with a slowdown game rather than trying to outgun Maravich, which a few teams actually did successfully:*

That was by design because Coach (Ray) Mears went into every game with a key. If there was a guy on the other team like Pete, the first goal was to shut him down. Coach Mears was on the NCAA Speaking Committee at the NCAA Tournament a year or two after I got out of school, and I was there because I was with Converse. He spoke first and he spoke about defense and how they had held Pete fifteen or sixteen points under his scoring average, and we won five out of six games against him. Then Adolph Rupp got up and said, "Well, we played Pete six times also and he averaged fifty-seven points against us, but we won all six." Everyone got a pretty good laugh out of that.

We used a chase defense with a box and one and the idea was to keep the ball out of his hands and don't let him get it back. We chased him with our point guard Billy Hann, who was almost Pete's size and had long arms. We double-teamed him until he gave it up and then Bill just fronted him so he couldn't get it back. It was kind of to the consternation of the UT fans. We were better than they were and we probably could have let him get his points and we still would have won, which is what the fans would have liked to see. When he was hitting twenty-eight points a game, he had a terrible night. What kind of pressure is that, where just to have an

average night you've got to get forty-five? Of course, we had
Tom Boerwinkle down low and he was a big seven-footer,
and Pete didn't get down in there against him. And our wing
players were really quick and he couldn't get away from
them, but I'll hand it to him because after that first game
against us he didn't force it.

He and I did a lot of yapping back and forth when playing each other. We were the original trash talkers. He had so
much publicity. When they came to Knoxville my junior
year, there had just been an article in *Sports Illustrated*,
which had been titled "The Coed Boppers' Top Cat," and
girls turned out like crazy when he came to town. They
called him "Cutie" around campus. Well, I called him that
the whole game, and finally he gets a breakaway—he wasn't
playing much defense and they had gotten a long rebound
and gotten the ball to him—and I was the closest guy to
him. He broke away, then stopped at the basket, turned
around, and waited on me, and before he put it in the basket
he said to me, "Here's two more for you, Cutie!" Then he
fouled out the next time down the floor and I brought it up
again as I followed him to the bench. It was always fun.

❧❧❧

*One other player who had the privilege of taking on
Maravich was Vanderbilt guard* **TOM HAGEN,** *and
part of the package deal was not striking up a
friendship among rivals:*

It was very interesting. One thing I take pride in was that we
never got beat by him. He was someone who other than a
hello or how ya doing he wasn't someone you could get
close to. He was somewhat aloof and arrogant. It wasn't like,
"Hey, Tom, how ya doin'," and "How are things going at
Vandy?" He was just kind of there to do his thing. But when
you looked at what he did he was such an entertainer, and
he was so innovative in what he did. I would watch his films
and try to learn moves. Bob Cousy was an innovator, but

Pete took it to another level. The behind-the-back passes and between-the-legs dribbling. He initiated a lot of that next-generation kind of moves.

We were a run-and-gun club and so were they, and he basically shot it whenever he could and however he could. One thing I remember was when we were down at LSU: It must have been about a five-point game toward the end and we were swapping baskets. He went up for a shot and somebody fouled him, but they didn't call it. As a result, he went over and grabbed the referee and acted like he was going to take a swing and hit him. Of course he didn't. But immediately that was a technical. I got the shot, hit it, and then we scored, and that put us up by eight, and that was pretty much the game. Those were the emotions that would come out from Pete.

We used a sort of floating zone against him. Played either a 2-3 or a 1-2-2, and then when Pete was in the zone, you would follow him, and we did a lot of switching off on him. You could double-team him when you could, and when he floated to another zone, that person floated with him until the next guy could pick him up. It made us focus on him rather than the team. You knew he was going to get up those twenty-five or thirty shots no matter what. So we would really focus on making sure you were on him and had a hand in his face when he came into our zone. And if he got by you, there had better be someone beside you to help out. Don't give him an open jump shot.

By the way, I learned the between-the-legs dribble from watching him on tape and then working in the gym by myself that summer.

Maravich's constant handling of a basketball, even away from the basketball court, sounds charming in retrospect, but it sometimes got on people's nerves, like his teammate **RICH HICKMAN,** *who roomed next door to the Pistol:*

I heard him banging on the walls every now and then. The only time we had words was when he would be bouncing a basketball and I was trying to sleep. It wasn't funny at the time, but it's like being in the army—you don't like being in the army at the time, but then you can look back and laugh about it. There were many nights when you could hear him banging something against the wall, and I think it was his head some of the time, not a ball.

It was easy for me playing with a superstar like Pete. When I was in high school, my best buddy was the guy who had gotten the publicity and all the glory—in fact, he ended up marrying my cousin. He was first team all-state and went to the Dapper Dan Classic, the whole bit. So I was kind of used to not being the main focus. I was out there doing what needed to be done. But when we got to be juniors and seniors, and recruits would come in—especially recruits who had been the big name in their own communities—it was a tough adjustment for some of those guys not being the focal point. We probably missed out on some recruits because they knew that Pete would get all the publicity. They couldn't handle it. We had some guys who came and left.

I was upfront with some of those guys, telling them, "You've got to realize that as long as he's here, there's a king-pin and then there's the rest of us. Get used to that, and if you have a hard time, you might want to look somewhere else, because I don't want to see you coming here and then jumping ship." It had been the similar deal for Tribbett because he had played high school basketball with Rick Mount. So we didn't have as much trouble with it as some of the other guys did. As far as I'm concerned, it was their loss. Getting to play with one of the greatest players ever was a pretty good deal.

It was a thrill. The guy was just fantastic to play with, but the thing is you had to stay on your toes. You never knew what to expect. By the time we were juniors, Jeff and I knew everything Pete was getting ready to do because we had played with him so much throughout the year. He made us better ballplayers because we were always on alert.

≈≋≋≈

In this day and age of sixty-four teams going to the NCAA Tournament and the occasional sub-.500 team that gets in for winning its conference postseason tournament, it's hard to imagine that in his day, Maravich never played in an NCAA Tournament game. Tournament fields were much smaller then and only one team per conference got in, and with Kentucky in tow, every other SEC team usually was playing for the silver medal. The Tigers finished the 1969–70 season, Maravich's senior season, 22-8 and yet all they got for such a good season was a bid to the NIT, which, however, was a more prestigious tournament then than it is today. **DONALD RAY KENNARD,** *LSU's athletic academic adviser at the time, recalls LSU's trip to the Big Apple in 1970 as a time for Maravich to shine— some of the time, anyway:*

We get to the NIT and are staying at the New Yorker Hotel. We check in and about an hour after we get there, we've got a press conference. So we go to the press conference, and it's the likes of Howard Cosell and Frank Gifford, and Curry Kirkpatrick, and Red Auerbach, and Tommy Heinsohn. I mean, the room was full, and there had even been a request from the Johnny Carson Show for Pete to go on. Pete was a celebrity, a household name. First question out of the box comes from Cosell: "Pete, how popular are you with the girls? Who are you dating? How many girlfriends you got?" "Mr. Cosell, I don't want to be rude with you, but that's personal and I don't want to discuss it. If there's any other questions, you can ask, but I'm not going to talk about my personal life."

Anyway, we went to Madison Square Garden and practiced, then we went back to the New Yorker. After dinner,

Press said, "Now look, guys, this is not a hick town. Y'all have never been to New York, and I don't want some of you to end up in the bottom of the Hudson River tomorrow. I want you to be very careful about what you do." Then he said, "Pete, here's a hundred dollars. It's this simple, don't spend it all tonight. You keep some of it. Now y'all know we're going to be a little lax on the curfew, so you guys just be careful because this is New York City and anything can happen to anybody in this town. It's a great town, one of the greatest towns in the United States, but you guys be careful because we're up here to play a bb game. OK?"

So, it's off to Broadway Joe's. We go to breakfast the next morning and Press said, "Pete, what about that one hundred dollars?" "Daddy, I don't have it." "Don't have it—what do you mean? I bet you spent it all at Broadway Joe's." "No, I didn't. They wouldn't let me buy anything there." "Okay, Pete, you don't have the hundred dollars?" "No, I don't have the hundred dollars."

We were practicing that afternoon around three o'clock, when a security guard came up to me and said, "Sir, there is some man out here on street level demanding to see Pete Maravich. He wants to meet him." I said, "Well, practice is closed and we have to close practice because of who Pete is and the draw that he is. Absolutely no one is admitted to practice, except for maybe a parent." The guard goes away and then comes back and says, "The man says that he has something that you or the Maraviches would want, and he wants to come into practice, so I think you had better come and talk to the man."

So I got out there to the man and introduce myself. I then learn from him that what had happened the night before was that when Pete had gotten out of his cab, this man was waiting to catch a cab to somewhere in New York, and when he got into the cab he saw a wallet on the seat, and it was Pete Maravich's wallet. He said to me, "Here's a wallet with a hundred-dollar bill in it. Do you think I could go in to practice and I could meet Maravich and get his autograph?"

And I said, "Sir, you are welcome to come in." And Press, who called me X-Ray, says, "X-Ray, what do you want?" And I said, "Coach, do you see that man standing over there? That hundred-dollar bill that Pete had in his wallet—he's got his wallet." Now if that had been Donnie Ray Kennard or John Doe, they probably never would have gotten their wallet back. "All this guy wants is to shake Pete's hand and get an autograph." Now anyone would have known that the LSU team was staying at the New Yorker, but this guy knew to come to Madison Square Garden to find the team practicing. Smart guy.

∞∞∞

DANNY YOUNG, *LSU student and sports information department assistant, often traveled with the team, giving him all kinds of access to Maravich the person as well as Maravich the player, and in both instances there was plenty to remember:*

I knew Pete well. I would keep assists at the game and a lot of times Pete would kid me, saying things like "I had more assists than that." The situation with Pete was such that we good-naturedly kidded each other. I was the one on road trips when Bud (Johnson) didn't go. I would have to set up the interviews and take Pete to the TV stations or meet with the newspaper people, and everyone wanted to interview him. There was an on-and-off policy depending on the mood of the coaches about when Pete could be interviewed. Press didn't like him being interviewed before games, but there were times that he would relax that. Like the time we went to North Carolina, which is where they were from. He allowed Pete a lot of latitude there because they were, in effect, going back home, so we did several TV interviews on the day of the game, which was unusual. We also did a trip to Oregon one time where he allowed a lot of stuff. Then it was on to L.A. and Hawaii. That was probably the classic road trip of all time.

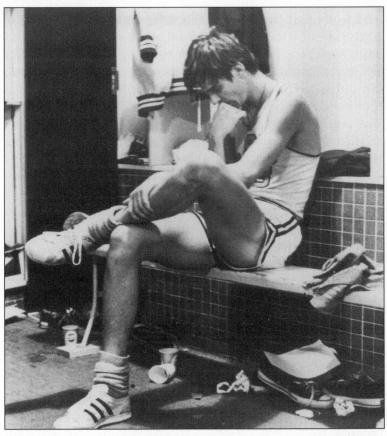

AP/Wide World Photos.

Pete never played on a championship team in college or the pros, and he usually took losing pretty hard. This photo shows a pensive Pistol Pete in the locker room after a highly touted, late-season loss to Kentucky in March 1970.

We played Clemson in Charlotte, and Pete was twenty-two of thirty from the floor and had a big night, and then we ran into a big snowstorm trying to get from North Carolina to Oregon. We wound up having to go to Atlanta, where we had to walk across the tarmac in the snow to get to another plane to go to Dallas, and then finally on to Oregon. And we played there two nights later, and that was the game in which Pete set the NCAA record for free throws (thirty of thirty-one in LSU's 76-68 victory over Oregon State). Their attitude was to foul him every time he had the ball, and when they fouled him he would make them.

There were something like seven players ejected from that game and there were fights all over the place. The crowd was ready to lynch us. The police had to come and get around the LSU team so we could get on the bus. The next night we played UCLA at Pauley Pavilion when they had one of their really good teams. They killed us (133-84). Pete had an average night (thirty-eight points, seven assists). We were exhausted. Everyone wanted to interview Pete that night, and that was at a time they were making a big deal about how Pete was supposedly the whole team, but he still won them over with his ballhandling.

⊰⊱

One of **DONALD RAY KENNARD**'s *favorite memories of a great Maravich moment is vividly etched in his mind because it occurred on his daughter Robin's seventh birthday:*

It was February 7, 1970. We celebrated her birthday that morning before I went to Alabama because I knew I was going to be late. We were going to be the opposing team for the opening of their new arena at Tuscaloosa. We flew over that Saturday afternoon and arrived in Tuscaloosa at three o'clock. Alabama is known for what? Football. Bear Bryant, right? Basketball was just a necessary sport to be a member of the NCAA. Well, when we flew over the campus that day coming in, we looked down and saw a double line a fourth of a mile long waiting for the ticket office to open, to see the magician. I don't know if Bear was in line.

We go to the new arena and get dressed and all. Pete got only sixty-nine that night and when the game was over, I was the first guy on the court, and he picked me up and hugged me and swung me around. I have seen him make moves that made me think of a monkey with a coconut. Pete was the consummate basketball player. It's so sad he never ended up winning a world championship.

⋙⋘

One of Pete's newfound acquaintances during his time in Baton Rouge was former LSU and Green Bay Packers football star Jim Taylor, who, although about ten years older than Maravich, later befriended the young Pistol, as **BUD JOHNSON** *remembers well:*

The two guys that worked hardest in the off-season were Jim Taylor and Pete Maravich, and it showed. When Pete first came to Baton Rouge in the late spring of 1966, June or July, I guess, he said, "I don't see anybody playing ball." I said, "Pete, not many people are going to play on a hot outdoor court in ninety-five-degree heat." Next day in the middle of the day, I saw Pete on a concrete court. He was challenging the heat, proving he could do it. He was by himself. You see, I had told him nobody does that in the heat of the summer, playing basketball on an outdoor court, so he had to prove he could do it.

Jim Taylor throughout his years in the pros, and even today, had a workout regimen that was just unbelievable. Ironically, the two were neighbors when Pete was playing for the Jazz, and they entered some of those Ironman competitions the networks come up with. *Superstars*. He and Jim Taylor both entered some of those things. They worked out together and ran on the levee.

Pete matured late. Not only was he a very skinny kid, he did not dunk the ball until his fifth year in the pros. He didn't start lifting weights until after his junior year in college. He got serious about weights not when he was in Atlanta, but when he was with the Jazz. His second year with the Jazz, when he was team captain and the first year he made all-pro, he was in the best shape of his life. That's when he first dunked the basketball.

An early basketball player who was a lifter was Bob Pettit. There was a weightlifting guru in Baton Rouge by the name of Alvin Roy, and he started Billy Cannon on them, then Jim Taylor and Bob Pettit. As a result, Bob went from being a frail, back-to-the-basket college center to an all-NBA power forward. One thing weightlifting does for an athlete, other than giving him strength, is to give him confidence. You could see that transformation in the early years of Pettit playing for Saint Louis. He was much more of an athlete as a pro than he had been in college. Taylor certainly didn't lack for impressions. And Pete in his second year with the Jazz really blossomed into his own. He was a leader and in the best shape of his life. His attitude was right. He wanted to win, and I think his workout regimen, when living near Jimmy Taylor, was such that he had never been in better physical condition. He had always been a pretty confident guy, but that accelerated the growth of his confidence when it came to handling the ball or doing passes.

〜

TAYLOR, who became a free agent after the Packers' first Super Bowl season of 1966, ended his career with the New Orleans Saints and while playing for the Saints settled into Metairie, Louisiana, for a number of years, where he became one of Maravich's neighbors during the mid-seventies when Pistol Pete was playing for the New Orleans Jazz, although they had met years earlier when Pete was still playing at LSU and getting ready to go into the pros:

I had met his dad and had talked to Pete a little bit when he was still at LSU. We got to be friends a little bit, but never really good friends. I talked with him a little bit when he was discussing getting his first pro contract, stuff like that. Casual friends, I would say. We might go over and play a few sets of tennis and then go somewhere and have a couple of beers and talk about competing and challenges and work habits and things like that, as well as how he got into basketball with his dad. We had some things in common we talked about, like what it meant to work hard and compete against tough players. We had different personalities. He really had some tremendous work habits to accomplish what he did. Even though he had a lot of talent, it still took a lot of hard work and perseverance to get that 90 to 95 percent level of capability, and he certainly achieved that at LSU, considering all those points he scored and the way he played.

I met Pete soon after he came to LSU in 1966. I left the Packers after the 1967 Super Bowl and then joined the Saints for one year before retiring. I built a home there, and he and his family bought a home across the street, about the time he left the Hawks to come play for the Jazz. Pete kind of stayed to himself, sort of like an introvert. He didn't like getting out in public and being around a lot of people. He wasn't real sociable. We were friends, but not like we saw each other two or three times a week. Just occasional friends. We'd play some sets of tennis at the beach club just a couple of blocks away. We both were very competitive. He had wonderful hand-eye coordination and was very talented. When he retired, he moved over to Covington, which was about the same time I was moving back to Baton Rouge.

3

THE PROS, AND
POETRY IN MOTION

Pete Maravich never averaged forty points or more in a season in the pros—not even close. But two important aspects of his ten-year National Basketball Association (NBA) career that did closely mirror his days and nights at LSU were his undisciplined, perhaps compulsive lifestyle and playing for teams that had trouble winning, let alone making the playoffs or winning league titles. Had Maravich been drafted by the "right" team—say, the L.A. Lakers or the Phoenix Suns, where his creative-playmaking ways would have meshed nicely with an established team (he probably never would have fit in with the Boston Celtics)—this story could have been totally different.

Instead, Maravich got drafted by a veteran team of disdainful, even envious players who didn't really want him (the Atlanta Hawks) and then traded to an expansion team of disassembled tinker-toy parts (the New Orleans Jazz) that regarded Maravich mostly as a seat-filler, prime-time thriller. In both places, Pistol Pete couldn't really go anywhere but sideways, because "up" was unattainable considering both sets of circumstances and "down" was already in place in New Orleans.

To his credit—bad knees, hangovers, hateful teammates, Type-A-personality coaches, and all—Maravich did pretty well in the pros, considering. He averaged 24.2 points during his career, led the league in scoring once (1976–77, at 31.1 points a game), was named to four all-NBA teams, and even got to play for the Boston Celtics part of one season, although his days in Beantown were pretty much spent as a pine-time observer. Maravich ended the 1979–80 season, his last NBA season, mostly wearing his warm-ups with the Celtics. He retired during the Celtics' 1980 training camp, just a day or two after scoring thirty-eight points in a preseason game. That doesn't quite compare to Ted Williams hitting a home run in his last at-bat in Boston, but it's not bad. Poetic injustice: The Celtics went on to win the NBA title in 1980–81, as Maravich missed his last chance to win a championship ring.

❈❈❈

MARAVICH, *on life with the Hawks while his life around him was falling apart, to include his dad's worsening situation as LSU coach and the deterioration of his mother's health—all while playing on a team for which he was not really a good fit:*

The years in Atlanta can only be described as a very dark time for me—a time of searching, a time of trying to be the best basketball player I could in a confusing and turbulent situation. . . . I was a self-proclaimed, self-made loner. As the isolation grew between the Hawks and me, a solitary life became even more the norm. All my life I had tried to find satisfaction from other people and gain acceptance, but after years of searching for approval the energy to do so began wearing me down.[1]

❈❈❈

MARAVICH, *on joining the Atlanta Hawks in 1970–71 for his rookie NBA season:*

The skepticism was just the beginning of ego trouble found so often in the world of sports. Atlanta was coming off a terrific year that saw them win the Western Division, and every player from the championship team was returning for another shot at the crown. For me to get adequate playing time, someone was going to have to ride the bench for a while. Economics alone would pressure coach Richie Guerin to start me.

The rumbling started subtly. A rumor circulated that the rookies as well as the veterans would be out to work me over on the court and make me earn my salary the hard way. I still wasn't full of bulk, and a few good blows could do considerable damage. But the threats never evolved, leading some to believe that team officials wanted me protected, apparently spreading the word that abusing the new acquisition was unpardonable.[2]

⧉⧉

As the newest, actually, the first, millionaire on the NBA block and with a reputation of shooting thirty or forty times a game, Maravich went to the Hawks in 1970 and ran into a nest of resentment. Atlanta was a veteran team that had won the Western Division the year before, and to someone like scoring guard **LOU HUDSON,** *Maravich as a new teammate had its pros and cons:*

I was already there when Pete came to the team and, personally, I looked forward to him coming to the team and meeting him and seeing who was the better player. He was a good guy with a good heart. Initially, he was a little standoffish and there were some adjustment problems where everyone had to adjust how they played. But even though our normal system was disrupted, I enjoyed playing with him.

With him coming in, there was a question of how the chemistry would be affected. On top of that, you're talking about a new guy coming in who would be making more money than everyone else put together, when in the past there had been talk that the team couldn't afford the players. We had lost a good player in Lenny Wilkens, who ended up being a Hall of Famer, because they couldn't pay him. So Pete comes along and suddenly they had the money to pay him. But that said more about the team than it said about Pete.

You also have to consider that he was a rookie and we were veterans, so there wasn't a whole lot of buddy-buddy contact. You've got to earn your stripes. It wasn't like, "Hey, everybody, Pete's here, let's go have a party and welcome him." It was pretty much the same treatment everyone else got and that was to make judgments on merit. At the same time, we had John Vallely who had been an all-American at UCLA. Both had been first-round picks. That was the big competition initially and the friction was between those two, and a few of the other guys.

I had come onto the team several years earlier under similar circumstances, as a first-round draft choice, but in my case I came along at a time when a player had just retired. I was replacing Cliff Hagan. In that case, I wasn't competing with an established veteran for his position. I was competing with other people for a position that was now open. It just so happens that Cliff had been in one of the scorer's spots, so they didn't have to change the offense to accommodate me. It was a good fit. The same plays they were running for Cliff they ran for me. It was a smooth transition.

Even then, however, there was some resentment because with a guy who scored retiring, there were veterans on the team who were thinking, Now I get a chance to get the ball. The guys weren't real happy to see me because I was a shooter. Once I earned the respect of the players, it was okay, although that took a while. There are established cliques when you get to a pro team, and if that's broken up and you seem to be the reason that's broken up, there's going to be some hidden reaction. There are dynamics you have to deal with when you come in as an outsider.

I really can't say how close we were to winning the NBA championship when Pete arrived. We took the Lakers to seven games in the Western Conference finals, when the Lakers had Chamberlain, West, Baylor, and Goodrich. Pete's thing was more complicated because when he came in, the team rules changed, things like everyone had gone through as rookies, what I guess you would call rookie-harassment rules. That stuff was waived when Pete came, and there was resentment with that, too, because all of the guys on the team who had come there as rookies had gone through that. When Pete came, it was suddenly no more rookies carrying the bags and that kind of stuff. Thing is, he didn't want to do it. He didn't want to do the traditional things a rookie did because everywhere he went there was a crowd of press to meet him. The initial reaction with the rest of us was that we had to do that stuff, so why doesn't he have to do it? It was Maravich who decided this.

And then the press was involved with the whole transition deal. Pete would say that we didn't like Pete, when the reality was that that didn't have anything to do with it. Pete would go out to dinner with us, and this was during segregation, but it was a transition period for segregation, too. One of his favorite deals was closing restaurants that wouldn't serve black people. He liked doing that and I did, too, at first, until it got to where I was the one getting his feelings hurt every time. And you're not talking about just a fifteen-minute ordeal. You're talking about going to the restaurant and going through the process. We would go to restaurants in the South—and even in the North sometimes—they wouldn't serve the black players. Pete liked to force the issue with restaurants because all of a sudden he had the power. He had the juice and he enjoyed doing that. It was a bold thing for him to do at the time, because he was putting himself out there, saying, "If you're not going to serve my friend, then you can't serve me either." That was a noble thing for him to do, but then he found a way to make it a game. Still, the people did learn a lesson because then the feds would come along and close the restaurant.

❧

Another key ingredient in the mix with the Hawks was player-coach **RICHIE GUERIN,** *a hard-nosed, old-school guard who favored chest passes to the between-the-legs stuff, and Hudson recalls that as an interesting combination with the freewheeling Maravich playing for the buttoned-down Guerin:*

Richie sort of put himself at risk, too, because Richie was a player-coach, and as a player-coach you sort of bond with your players, but all of a sudden you become general manager and player-coach; it really strained all the relationships. When he did things that involved Pete, everything would be perceived by the rest of us as personal because we were not only teammates, but friends. But when Richie put his GM hat on, you had a problem and the whole concept was tainted with all this stuff going on at the same time.

I probably wasn't as reactionary to all this stuff as some of the players were, because with Pete, it became the Pete and Lou Show. He was excited that we were doing all the Jerry West and Elgin Baylor stuff like total scoring by two players, and he would find out about a record and he would say, "I've got to get so many points and you've got to get so many points, and I've got to get you the ball." As a player, I didn't have a problem with that. He liked it because it would put him in the record books again.

When Cotton (Fitzsimmons) came in as the coach, things changed and the whole team was rearranged. Joe Caldwell and Zelmo Beaty went to the ABA, and Bill Bridges was traded to Philadelphia for Jim Washington. So the team that had come to Atlanta from Saint Louis was not the team Pete was on once we made the transition. And the winning went away. As I look back, Pete was sort of a distant buddy. He was not a real warm, fuzzy person you got to know well. With him being down in New Orleans later on, and then when he was born again and turned into a vegetarian and all that sort of stuff, that was extreme stuff for that time.

*In coming to the Hawks in 1971 in the trade that sent Bill Bridges to the 76ers, **JIM WASHINGTON** was joining the Hawks for the second time. He had originally been drafted by them in 1965, when they were still in Saint Louis, and so in some ways he was the newcomer in much the same way that Maravich had been earlier:*

Pete's and my relationship was a pretty close one. We spent time together off the court and on the road, whether it was eating breakfast or whatever the case may be. In fact, we all got along together well, which I understand hadn't been the case the year before I got there. There had been some jealousy and resentment with his coming in and signing the big contract and all that stuff. I don't think our friendship was a matter of my intentionally reaching out to him. As far as animosity among the players, there may have been some things said on the court in the heat of competition, but off the court everyone got along pretty well.

When we were playing on the road, Pete and I usually got something to eat together, and we liked to do a lot of the same things. He was very outgoing. I think he wanted to be accepted, to be just one of the guys. But he was still a kid, kind of wild at the time and liked to have fun. Like most of these guys coming into the league now, there's an adjustment period, and he was adjusting to life as an NBA basketball player and the fact that it wasn't the same kind of life he had been living at his alma mater. He wasn't the guy who was going to lead the league in scoring; he was just another one of many very good basketball players.

I would imagine there was a certain amount of insecurity on his part, and again, I wasn't with the Hawks when he got there. But I know Richie Guerin. I had played for Richie my first year as he was player-coach for the Saint Louis Hawks when I came into the league, and he was one of the guards from the old school. He was very tough, so I would imagine having a guy like Pete Maravich under his tutelage was an interesting experience.

Richie was very competitive and a tough guard, productive in his own way. I can remember him scoring thirty points in a game against the Lakers after being out of the league for two years, so that gives you an idea of what kind of a competitive player and person he was. And he did it with the old-style play, and here Pete comes and he's just the opposite. The passes would come from all kinds of directions, and the press here made it appear that it was the other players' fault when they didn't catch his passes. Richie felt a lot of times the pass could have been more standard, and the fact we weren't wining ball games didn't help.

You've got to understand professional players. Pete came to a team with two guys on the team who had established themselves and been recognized by their peers as all-stars— Lou Hudson and Walt Bellamy—and so if anything, they probably thought any adjustment that had to be made needed to be made by Pete toward them, not the other way around. When you're not wining ball games, you have to prove yourself that what you bring to the club was beneficial, and that wasn't the case here. Pete was a very productive player as an individual, but we were not productive as a team and as a member of the team, each player has to share a part of the blame.

⊗≈≋≈⊗

TOM BOERWINKLE, *one of Maravich's old SEC foes, was by now playing for the Chicago Bulls and felt some empathy for Pistol Pete, except of course when it was time for the Bulls to play the Hawks:*

As I recall his time in Atlanta was kind of a tough time. He was down there with a bunch of veteran ballplayers and he was kind of the new slick kid on the block. They didn't accept him very well right away. Everyone thought he was going to come into the NBA and right away score forty or fifty points a game. He had to force a lot of shots. The other thing is, when playing with a player that good with a basketball, it takes a while to get used to him. You can be there wide open and still not expect a ball to be coming and bouncing off your head. It was an older veteran team. Those were all great established, quality NBA players—all-stars probably, every one of them. If you don't shoehorn him in there somewhere, the fans go crazy. So it puts the coach and the organization in a real precarious situation, and now you're making a lot of great players take a second seat.

One of the greatest matchups of all time in my book was Jerry Sloan (a Bulls teammate of Boerwinkle's) guarding Pete Maravich. Jerry was probably the most determined defensive guard in the NBA, and Jerry had tremendous pride. He played Pete Maravich heads up and never gave an inch. Jerry wasn't real fast or real quick and wasn't real strong, but he was the last guy you ever wanted to get into a fight with. He was always going to the floor, diving over tables—the hardest player I could ever think of in the NBA. He knew he was a little short on talent, so he knew he had to give a little more in the effort area, and he did every night.

The matchups between him and Pete Maravich were classic. They were worth the price of admission. Jerry would meet Pete across halfcourt and just get in his face and not let him go. If you had talked to Pete and asked him, "Who was the one guy you didn't want to see on the other team when you walked on the basketball floor?" he probably would have said, "Number 4 wearing a Bulls jersey."

Jerry was such a determined athlete that he would go to (Dick) Motta and say, "Hey, I'm going to guard him," and it was the right matchup because Jerry was six-five, and Pete about six-six. Both were kind of rawboned kids, totally different in their skills areas—Pete's were on offense, and Jerry's were defensively. But I mean to tell you, in my book—and they talk about Chamberlain and Russell and all the great matchups—but Jerry Sloan against Pete Maravich was a tough one to top. Jerry knew if he didn't take that approach and do that kind of job, Pete would embarrass him, although not intentionally. And Pete didn't back down—he went after him, but Jerry did an extremely good job on him.

⁐⁐⁐

*There was one familiar face on the Hawks when Pete joined the team coming out of LSU and that was **HERB WHITE**, his opposite number from Georgia. White had been picked in the eighth round and subsequently made the team, and it was only natural that he and Pete would become good friends, although it was an alliance that lasted only one year. White reinjured a knee he had hurt in high school, and he never played another season in the NBA:*

I thought I had seen the last of Pistol Pete—I was hoping, anyhow, after being about killed covering him in games. Then I get drafted by the Hawks and now had to guard him in practice every day for about a year. It was kind of tough. We roomed together on the road and lived in the same apartment complex here in Atlanta. We had a lot of good times together, kind of wild. Nothing like it is now with celebrities and superstars, but he was about the biggest thing to come along back then, no doubt about it. Everywhere we went it was a mob scene.

A lot of times on the road people would call the room, and often it was some young lady who wanted to meet Pistol Pete. I would just answer the phone and say, "Well, c'mon up." Or "I'll meet you in the bar," and all they knew was that he was a white guy with a mustache and brown hair, and I fit that description. I remember one night, our second or third time going around the league, about midseason, Pete and I were sitting around and he said, "You know, it's the most amazing thing. I keep telling them who I am and they don't believe me. They say, 'I've already met Pistol Pete.'" I just kind of turned my head and looked away.

Richie Guerin was a defensive-minded guy and that was my thing, I played strong defense. Richie was a tough old-school guy and it was a clash of personalities, although I think Pete really respected Richie and I think Richie liked Pete. He was trying to change his style because the Hawks were a veteran team, a veteran black team for that matter that had been together for quite a while. So you have Pete coming in and getting all that money and people proclaiming him the next greatest thing to hit the league, it created a tough situation.

Joe Caldwell decided to leave because he wanted the bigger contract, to get the same kind of money. And he was a great player—the heart and soul of the Hawks at that time. Then Bridges held out in training camp for a little while. I couldn't really blame those guys, but then again, the Hawks were in a tough situation because we played at Georgia Tech in Alexander Memorial Coliseum, which only held about sixty-four hundred people, and here they are already paying Pete all this money, and they were limited to what they could bring in. It led to a lot of resentment and it was a very turbulent year. Pete was a likable guy off the court, but some people really resented him. Walt Hazzard and he didn't get along that well, and Walt was the point guard on the team. But I could understand Walt's position some, too. The fact that we made the playoffs was unbelievable. You can attribute that to Richie Guerin and his coaching ability.

The other guys didn't really rough Pete up in practice because Richie wasn't going to put up with that. But we had a lot of team meetings where people would try to say what was on their minds and talk it out, trying to get things together. A lot got aired out, but things didn't change a whole lot. Pete would try, then he would revert back to doing his old kind of stuff. Pete and I used to talk a lot about it because Pete was my roommate on the road, and I would listen to him and say, "Well, man, you've got to play your game and try to do your best, and you've got to play some defense because that's what Richie wants you to do." Pete could play defense because he had quick reactions and he had those long arms, it's just that he never had before. He didn't play any defense in college, so he didn't have the fundamentals and that made it even more of a difficult situation.

It was a dichotomy for Pete. They had brought him in to bring people in, so they wanted a little bit of Showtime, but they were trying to blend him into the team, too. He tried to become a team player at the same time they were expecting him to do some great things for them. It really, really bothered him. Down deep, he wanted to win more than anything else. Playing for his father in college and in that circus atmosphere they played in wasn't conducive to him. It probably hurt him.

Pete did do some of the rookie initiation stuff, but probably not as much as the rest of us. I don't think any of those guys would ever do anything to hurt Pete or the team. Walt Hazzard came closest to that. I think they kind of resented Pete because they blamed him for Caldwell leaving. For a while there they had Pistol Pete and Dr. J. They thought they had the rights to Dr. J when he jumped leagues, but he ended up going to Philadelphia. Now that would have been something.

I hear a lot of guys nowadays trying to compare Jason Williams at Sacramento to Pistol Pete. The guy is amazing, no doubt about it, and he can do some things with the basketball that I never saw Pete do, but what people don't realize now is that you're allowed to carry the ball, and walk with the ball, and do stuff like that. If Pete hadn't had to keep his hand on top of the ball like we had to back then, he would have done the same things that Jason is doing. Guys are taking it further these days, doing stuff and experimenting.

❈

Sometime after Cotton Fitzsimmons had replaced Guerin as the Hawks' coach, Maravich finally got exasperated enough to tell the coach off, as recalled by a former NBA player requesting anonymity:

Pete hated Cotton Fitzsimmons. One time Cotton got him so ticked off, he said, "Cotton, if you don't watch it, I'm going to pick you up and stuff you into a pillowcase." Pete said, "I swear I said that to him."

❈

*Maravich at times lived life on the edge, when something as supposedly routine as a drive to the airport could be like a ride in the space shuttle with Pete behind the wheel, as **HERB WHITE** found out on several occasions while living in the same Atlanta apartment complex with Pete. One way or another, they always managed to draw attention:*

We used to come out to our cars after the games and women would just leave notes and telephone numbers on our windshields. Pete had bought this—I guess he had a little redneck in him, and where most players had Mercedes and Jaguars and stuff like that—well, Pete had gotten him a brand-new Plymouth Road Runner with a 452 in it and a green alligator roof. He was just notorious for stuff like that. We would take turns driving to the airport, and when it was his turn, he was invariably late. Our plane would be leaving in twenty minutes and it would be twenty minutes to the airport, and he would pull up in the apartment parking lot and go, "Let's go, man." We would just haul butt in that Road Runner about 110 miles an hour all the way to the airport. He was just crazy.

❈

*Everyone has a great Maravich story, and one of **WHITE**'s favorites is the time he and Pete managed to* *get a male passenger thrown off an airplane flight they were getting ready to take:*

This was back in 1970 or 1971, around the time there had been that thing with D. B. Cooper jumping out of an airplane with all that money and some hijackings. There seemed to be a rash of that stuff going around. We were out on the West Coast and were getting ready to take a late flight, something like San Diego to San Francisco, I don't remember exactly. I hated flying and it didn't really bother Pete.

We were sitting in the airport like at one or two in the morning, and I guess we weren't going to be playing the next day because we were drinking beer. Pete got to talking to some guy next to him on the other side from me—just some businessman, I guess, because he had a business suit on. I wasn't paying that much attention, but Pete liked talking to people, especially if they didn't know who he was. You get tired of people coming up to you to talk about basketball. He just liked to shoot the breeze. After a while I could see that the guy was getting real kind of strange. He started talking about how, "Oh, I'm a failure. I've let my family down and I haven't been successful and the best thing is for me to just be dead." Really some dramatic strange stuff.

A couple minutes later, it's time to go catch our flight. So we pay our tab and go on walking down to the gate. We're standing in line fixing to get on the plane, when I happen to turn around and notice this same guy standing in our line waiting to get on, too. He was still crying and upset. So me and Pete get on the plane, and we're sitting up near the front of the plane. I turn to Pete and say, "You know that guy you were talking to in the bar is going to be on this flight, and I bet this guy is planning to blow up the plane or something because he had been talking about wanting to die, maybe to get insurance for his family." So we end up talking ourselves into a frenzy. So the guy comes along down the aisle and passes us, and he looks shaky, really messed up. He goes back toward the back of the plane where he finally sits down, and we're wondering what we should do. Should we go tell somebody? We walk back there and tell Richie (Guerin) what's happening, and he says, "You guys are out of your mind." Richie was tough as nails and didn't want to hear that stuff.

So we went back and sat down, and I'm looking back there and I see that guy, and by now I know that guy is a potential danger. So we got a stewardess and told her what happened in the bar and what the guy was saying. She went walking back there to check the guy out. Then she comes hauling butt up the aisle, and by this time the plane has pulled away from the gate and we're starting to head out to the runway. She went up and knocked on the cockpit door, and a couple moments later, I guess it was the copilot came walking back and spent some time talking to the guy, then he walks back, and next thing I know we're pulling back into the gate, and the captain comes on and says, "We're going to pull back into the gate for a minor problem."

So they pull up to the gate and a couple of security people come in and take the guy off the plane. Then, they were afraid he had a bomb in his luggage or something, so then they had to search all the luggage on the whole damn plane to find his bags. So we were there like an hour and a half and everybody is ticked off and Richie is yelling at Pete and me, "You two (jerks) are responsible for all this." I don't know whatever happened to the guy. Poor guy probably went home and killed himself after that. We had already had a couple emergency landings that year, and the guy was probably just having a bad day.

❧❧❧

*Maravich played four years with the Hawks and then was traded to the Jazz, bringing him back close to home in New Orleans, but the move certainly did nothing to improve his chances of winning an NBA championship ring. **BUD JOHNSON**, who had been LSU's sports information director when Maravich was* *there, now had a similar position with the Jazz, so he and Maravich were reunited, and the elapsed years gave Johnson a good perspective for comparing the young Maravich to the NBA version:*

One of the first things the Jazz did was trade for Pete. I guess when Pete saw me, he associated me with a lot of interviews, and he hoped he wouldn't have to go through that again. In other words, "Let's don't go through the amount of interviews we had at LSU." That was the feeling he expressed to management, and I was caught in the dilemma of the same thing I had encountered in Baton Rouge—the only way we were going to get any recognition was with him. We had an expansion ballclub, and what they were trying to do was get somebody who had a name because we were loaded up with players that were rejects from other ballclubs—part of being an expansion team. He did the same thing in New Orleans he had done in Baton Rouge. He turned the city on to basketball.

By now, Pete had become a more physical person, and was now over two hundred pounds. He had a neck and shoulders, and he had some definition. He became captain of the team his second year here, and also made the all-NBA team. He was now more of a team leader than just a guy looking for a shot. He was constantly challenging other players to get more out of their games. When the game got down to crunch time, he wanted the ball. It was a replay of LSU— no world beaters on either ballclub.

I remember a game against Cleveland. Bill Fitch is a helluva coach, and I loved to sit behind the visiting bench and hear somebody like Fitch tell the guys what to do in a time-out. There were about five or seven seconds left in the game, Jazz ball, and you think they're going to say something of consequence in the huddle, and I'm leaning forward so I can hear, and it was just like it had been with Mississippi State or Florida: "We've gotta stop him, we've gotta stop him." Same ol' thing. Pete gets the ball, drives the baseline, and lays it up. Game over.

Maravich, by this time with the Jazz, makes a move against the Golden State Warriors during the 1976–77 season. He led the NBA in scoring that season with an average of 31.1 points a game.

MARTY MULE, *a sportswriter with the* New Orleans Times-Picayune, *was a Jazz beat writer in those days and said there were two ways of looking at Maravich's value to the team, which as an expansion club full of over-the-hill veterans and the odd starting-caliber player, was then basketball's version of what the hapless New York Mets had been in the early sixties with players such as Marv Throneberry and an aging Richie Ashburn:*

There were two schools of thought then: one, that Pete was just a drawing card, and the other that he was a real aid to this team. To me, there was no way he wasn't a major contributor to the team. The night that he scored sixty-eight points against the Knicks will always stick out in my mind. For one thing, he put on an incredible shooting exhibition, and two, that was the only game that season he fouled out of. He fouled out with something like two minutes to go on a very questionable call, and if he hadn't fouled out, he would have scored seventy-five points. I remember that for two reasons. Once they called a time-out and he was trotting back to the bench and his teammates were all pumped up, jumping up and waving towels, and he was startled; it was like he didn't realize—he was so focused—the pace he was scoring at.

There were two other reporters and me sitting at press row watching the game and maybe about halfway through the first half, someone said, "I know there's something special happening here because you guys aren't sitting there and cracking jokes like you usually do and talking the whole time." We were mesmerized the whole time watching what was going on.

❧❧❧

MARAVICH, on finding ways to get his mind off the game, by which time he was playing for the New Orleans Jazz:

"UFO-ology" was one of the fads I got into to escape. I read everything I could get my hands on about UFOs, astronomy, and astrology, which led me into the fringes of the occult. I was intrigued with the possibility of life on other planets, and I remember thinking how nice it would be if creatures from another planet would come and take me away from it all. I know how off the wall I must have sounded, but I was looking for something to give me the inner peace I couldn't find within myself.[3]

⬥⬥⬥⬥

***JIM BARNETT** played half of that first season with the
Jazz before being traded away to the New York Knicks,
and remembers that first Jazz season as one of many
interesting angles, not all of them particularly positive:*

Scotty Robertson was the coach. I had broken my thumb
during a workout in September while I was still with the
Warriors, so I couldn't do anything for the Jazz in training
camp except run. Scotty installed what I used to call a kind
of shuffle offense—a modification of a triple post, actually.
I liked it and immediately flourished. It was my ninth year
in the league. Here's a good trivia question: Who was the
first player in Jazz history to score thirty points in a game?
It wasn't Pete. It was me. Three games in a row I had
twenty-five or more points, when Pete was having to miss
some games.

   We had about twenty veterans try out for this club, plus
there were two guys drafted that had guaranteed contracts.
So it was dog eat dog. Neal Walk was our center and we had
picked up Rick Roberson from the Lakers. Rick was a big
guy, but he was kind of lazy. Neal had once averaged twenty
points and fifteen rebounds for the (Phoenix) Suns, but now
his lifestyle was such that it wasn't conducive to remaining a
top NBA player by any stretch.

   Scotty Roberston got fired when we were 1-13 or 1-14,
and then we got Butch van Breda Kolff. Neal Walk drove him
bananas. Neal kind of went out there and floated around,
saying, "This is like ballet, an art form. We shouldn't even
keep score. We should just play for forty-eight minutes, not
keep score, and at the end of the game set up a little picnic at
halfcourt." One time we were in Cleveland where Neal had
scored like two points and gotten three rebounds in twenty-
eight minutes, and we got clocked. So we're sitting in the
locker room after the game and Butch walks by really
steamed and Neal goes, "Hey, Butch, relax. The sun's going
to come up tomorrow."

The permed 'do and semi-grin can't disguise the fact that Maravich is where he doesn't want to be, riding the bench. He spent the last few months of his career with the Celtics, finally retiring during the preseason in the fall of 1980.

It was a good blend of veterans and young guys, but the problem was that the veterans were just not good and the young guys weren't good enough either. We were a hodge-podge of a group; we had Pistol Pete and that was about it. There was a lot riding on him, but if you look at the attendance records, we were getting something like three and four thousand people a game, playing at Municipal Auditorium, and the locker room was on a stage behind curtains.

Then later on we went to another college that had a raised floor somewhere in between Tulane and New Orleans. Super Dome not built yet. Players Association people came down and said, "Hey, you can't play like this. It's too dangerous." We had played a couple of games and guys were falling off the raised floor. They put up a rope net through which people had to look to watch the game. It was kind of like what pro wrestling is. When people fell off the floor, they fell into these big rope nets. It was a bizarre atmosphere. One time we were playing there, van Breda Kolff was so upset at halftime that he took a chair and threw it toward the bathroom door and all four legs went through the door and it just stuck there.

I got the feeling that Pete wanted to win, but he was very philosophical about it and he didn't seem to mind losing that much. He was kind of a happy-go-lucky guy. He made $700,000 that year and I had just gone over $100,000 a year. David Thompson got a contract that year for $3.2 million for four years. Nobody made half a million dollars a year before that, I don't think. Maybe not even $400,000, except probably for Wilt (Chamberlain). That was big money back in 1974. I was making $110,000 cash and I was very happy. Pete screwed around a lot when he played, even though he played hard. When I left we were like 4-42, but they did a lot better after my trade.

⚬⚬⚬

MARAVICH, *on his health and eating habits, which he changed drastically sometime after he started playing with the Jazz:*

Ever since I was a little eighth grader I found myself constantly having to overcome sickness or injury to play basketball. Even in the pros I had had to overcome mononucleosis and Bell's palsy. I could never figure out why I was always getting sick, but I did know that my health was definitely standing in the way of reaching my full potential. I didn't see anything wrong with the way I ate because I was like most Americans who loved to eat a juicy steak or grab a hamburger and fries on the run. Eventually, I decided to take the advice of a fellow player (from a previous team) who was into natural foods. He seemed to never be sick and always went the whole season without injury. On his recommendation, my new diet consisted of fruits, vegetables, fish, and some chicken. I had red meat maybe once or twice that year, but for the most part I stuck to a natural food diet free from salt and sugar. I couldn't believe how great I gradually began to feel. My new diet combined with lifting weights gave me energy that I had never known.[4]

❦

BARNETT *got along well with Maravich in part because he found Pistol Pete to be selfless, at least off the court:*

During training camp, we played all over in places like Monroe, Louisiana. One night, and Pete wasn't married at this time, we saw this very striking girl who was about our age. We were eating in a hotel restaurant, about three or four of us, and I had seen her earlier making a phone call. We see her again at the restaurant and Pete says to me, "Hey, Jim, if you're not going to go over and hit on her, then I'm going to." So he deferred and gave me first choice, which I thought was interesting. I went over there and everything worked out. So he gets credit for an assist on the play. I've always remembered that, and it was pretty unselfish.

In those days, chasing broads was the fifth quarter. Jack McMahon, my coach at San Diego, would be pleased if he saw you coming in at three with a girl with you, because he wanted his players to have fun and to be relaxed for the games. He'd give you a fist up and all that stuff, and the next day he wanted to know all the details. He thought that was part of the NBA.

I liked Pete. He was ahead of his time with that great ball control, and he had that flair. He didn't like doing things the conventional way. We were coming down once in a game, I think against the Washington Bullets, and I've got an easy lay-up, I mean an easy lay-up, so he does some kind of pass where he goes behind his back and with no look throws it over my head and into the stands, and that kind of ticked me off. He kind of got a sheepish grin on his face and said,

"Okay, I'll throw it to you right next time." You couldn't stay mad at him.

❧

The circumstances in which **BARNETT** *found out he had been traded were almost comical, and the story involved a bit of the happy-go-lucky side of Maravich:*

I got traded February 1, 1975, to the New York Knicks. I got a phone call right around midnight from a reporter for a Washington paper, and he said, "Hey, Jim, I want you to know they just consummated a trade, and you and Neal Walk were just traded to the New York Knicks for Henry Bibby, a number-one draft choice, and $100,000 cash, and Rick Adelman and Otto Johnson were traded to Kansas City for Nate Williams." So they traded the four of us for two players.

Next day at practice, no one says anything. The team still hadn't informed me or the other guys involved. I drove there with Rick (Adelman). I told him while driving we had been traded. So we go to Tulane University where we practice and we start warming up, and Coach (van Breda Kolff) doesn't say anything. We didn't mind doing a couple of little things, figuring he's going to tell us something. But then we realized he was going to get a full practice out of us before he told us anything. He couldn't practice with only eight players out of a twelve-man roster. I told Pete that we were traded and he said, "You're kidding."

After about ten or fifteen minutes, I finally go over to Butch and say, "Hey, Butch, why should we even be practicing if we're now on another team?" And with a (crap)-eating grin, he goes, "What do you mean?" And I said, "Well, I hear there's been a trade." And he said, "That may not be true. There's always rumors and that kind of stuff." So I said, "Okay, tell me." I told him about what the reporter had told me and asked, "Is it true?" He said, "It's true," and I say, "Practice is over." And Pete's out there on the court practicing a little bit on his own and listening with one ear and I said, "Hey, Pete, practice is over." And he throws the ball to the top of the gym and then starts shooting hook shots. Pete loved it because practice was over.

∞

BARNETT *was another NBA player who compared Maravich to a certain Boston Celtic:*

He was like Havlicek. If you turned your head, he could go without the ball. He would find a way to beat you with or without the ball. One time I was playing for the Warriors and he was playing for Atlanta. I had this reputation for being a little flaky. He had the ball and hadn't terminated his dribble. He was about thirty feet away and was looking to make a pass, looking to make some kind of play. I came up on him and I thought I would just try to perturb him, so I just ran up to him like some kind of nut and I bent over and stuck my head into his belly. And he laughed, didn't make a move, and said, "What in the hell are you doing?" He got a kick out of it, and he liked to laugh.

∞

*Maravich ended his pro career by finishing out the 1979–80 season playing for the Celtics. He retired in the fall of 1980 during training camp, thus missing out on one last chance for an NBA championship ring. The Celtics went on to win the title in 1980–81, although Maravich presumably didn't have any great regrets about not sticking around one more year, as longtime friend **BOB SANDFORD** pointed out:*

He wanted a championship more than anything in the world, until he became a born-again Christian. He could see the writing on the wall with the Boston Celtics. He knew he could contribute and he knew he could play, but he didn't think they were going to let him contribute. Basically, they had him on that team to keep him from going to Philadelphia. They brought him over there, and he was not the type of player who wanted to be on a team and get a ring by sitting on the bench. He wanted no part of that. That was not the kind of a championship ring he wanted, the kind that somebody just gives to you.

4

SHOWTIME

There still are many Pistol Pete wannabes roaming the countryside. Some are even trying to ply their trade in the NBA. Mention the name "Pete Maravich" in NBA circles these days, and the name that gets spit out most often is that of Jason Williams, the smallish white point guard for the Sacramento Kings. But labeling Williams a Maravich clone when it comes to all offensive facets of the game is as much a stretch as it would be trying to stretch his frame into Pistol Pete's six-foot-five—some will insist he was more like six-six—frame.

The hardest part in trying to describe Maravich's full range of ball skills to today's Generation X professional player is generational skepticism. If it's not on tonight's ESPN highlights package, then it doesn't exist. Then there's that whole deal of being from a different generation and trying to overcome a youngster's cynicism that what he is hearing is really the truth. "Yeah, right, Pops. That Pete Maverick guy was a real wizard, but he played in the Stone Age and couldn't cut it against today's offerings of the likes of Williams, Kobe Bryant, and Allen Iverson." Yeah, right.

Let's put it to you straight, folks: With today's wide-open brand of NBA basketball, the three-point line, and liberal interpretations of what constitutes a travel, a carry, or continuation, Maravich today would eat everyone's lunch. There would be no stopping him outside of the usual, dumbed-down mugging tactics and in a world where proficient outside shooting and creative passes—not the ego-gratifying, wasteful ones—border on extinction. Maravich was the original and genuine Showtime, an endlessly creative genius who could beat anyone one-on-one. Bring on Kobe and bring on Jason, and let's pass that rock to Dick Vitale, babeeee!

⚬⚬⚬

*Not every basketball fan is enamored of ESPN college basketball analyst **DICK VITALE**, but few can question his genuinely unbridled enthusiasm for the game, as well as an astute knowledge of the game's history. It's natural for a basketball junkie like Vitale to light up when talking about Maravich's skillful flair:*

I met Pistol a number of times, and I was always in awe when I spoke to him. I was always amazed with his talent level because I realized in talking to his dad how many hours he put in to be able to have that kind of control with a basketball. His control was as good as anybody's I've seen in my life. His wizardry, his passing ability, his skill level facing the kind of pressures he faced. He was a one-man concert tourist, like this Ricky Martin guy now, or Bruce Springsteen, Lionel Ritchie, and Tina Turner. They put on an unbelievable show and have the crowds in an unbelievable frenzy.

I just saw Faith Hill and Tim McGraw the other day, and the place was like they had them in the palm of their hand—and that is what Pistol did. I remember teasing him about that: "My God, man, I wish I could have had one iota of the ball control that you had." Like when I go off to speak at functions, such as executives at Pepsi, I try to have control of that group with my microphone, and that's what Pete did with that basketball. All eyes were centered on him. You saw the floppy socks and you couldn't get your eyes off him, even when he didn't have the basketball. His movement without the ball to get his hands on the ball was incredible, because teams were stacking their defenses against him.

It would be unreal, unreal, to think what this guy would have scored with a three-point line. He would have been so difficult to defend, because he was so difficult to defend as it was. He would have eaten that line, especially at the collegiate level. His last year with the Celtics, I was coaching Detroit. He was at the end of his career, but he was still such a special guy and such a special talent. There was a tendency among people to become like the Kodak Man. That's where I got that term, almost because of guys like the Pistol and Calvin Murphy, where everybody else wants to stand around and take pictures, snapping photos while this guy was doing his thing. Between the legs, behind the back— just incredible!

⚮

HERB WHITE, *the former Georgia player who went from being Maravich foe to friend when they both played as NBA rookies with the Atlanta Hawks, credits Maravich with changing the face of basketball in the South:*

No doubt he revolutionized the game in the South. When I was with the Hawks, I taught him all different kinds of dunks. That was my thing. He could do a lot of different dunks but would never try them in a game. We would do all kinds of stuff in practice and before the games, and I asked him, "Why don't you try to dunk in the games?" and he said, "I don't want to miss because I'd look bad." And I said, "Man, you've probably missed more shots than anyone in the history of basketball." And he said, "Yeah, but missing a dunk is different." And you're right about that.

⟨⟩

Maravich on becoming an instant celebrity early in his sophomore year at LSU:

This sudden leap to fame was a lot to handle. I had to balance my life between the insecure person I was and the carefree college prankster and athlete I wanted to be. Added to that, representing LSU everywhere I went carried more responsibility.

As a personal rule I wouldn't leave the arena after a game until every autograph seeker got my signature, which sometimes meant a two-hour delay getting home. I must admit I never really understood why people wanted autographs in the first place; I guess people looked to me as a hero. Webster defines a hero as a (person) noted for (his or her) special achievements. Hero is also defined as a long sandwich. Since a lot of people called me a hot dog during my career, either definition may have been the reason people wanted my autograph.[1]

⟨⟩

TOMMY HESS, one of Maravich's LSU teammates, admitted to being somewhat, as Vitale would describe, of a Kodak man:

Another thing, he was the only guy I ever saw throw a pass to himself off the backboard. He made a penetration to the goal, and he used to do that kind of stuff in practice a lot. Some of this stuff was just created on the run, ad-libbed. He worked on it. I saw him do it in practice and saw him do it in a game.

There was one time in particular against Tulane in a free-throw situation. This was something so elemental once you saw it, but when you see it for the first time, you think, Omigod! While the opposing team is shooting a free throw, one of our guys is sneaking his way back over the half-court line. Pete saw him out of the corner of his eye without tipping it off that he was seeing anything. The guy makes the free throw and Pete goes to take the ball out under the basket. Most guys would have stepped out, turned around, and thrown it deep with a football-type pass. Not Pete. With his back to the court, he walked out of bounds with the ball in his hands and, without turning around, flipped it back over his head—he froze everybody because it was totally ad-libbed, and no one knew that our guy was back there at the other end of the court. I think it was Jeff Tribbett. He caught it and put it in for a lay-up. He had incredible court awareness. It was more than just talent. Somebody like a Joe Montana or Steve Young knows where that defensive pressure is coming from, and that's what Pete had. He was absolutely amazing. He probably would have been a very good quarterback. He had great soft hands and great vision. I never saw him throw a football, but I saw him throw a Frisbee and he could throw it a mile.

✄

DAVE COWENS, *the future star center of the Boston Celtics through the seventies, played college ball at Florida State, and while he faced a Maravich-led LSU only once, he knew all about the Pistol even before they got to the pros. For another thing, they had worked together at Lefty Driesell's basketball camp in North Carolina:*

When it came to working with kids, he was like the Pied Piper, the same way it was for guys also like Calvin Murphy, who were exciting to watch. They were fun, full of life, and bigger than life. He was a Harlem Globetrotter type of player with legitimate game. He promoted the game of basketball with his style. He was never a really good defender. What he was was a showman, and he was a great showman. He was a great basketball player.

Jason Williams, that little guard from Sacramento, is a Pete wannabe, but he can't score like Pete Maravich. He can't attack the basket and get to the rim like Pete could. He's got a few fancy things here and there, but Pete had all that stuff as well as a substantial game to go with it. Remember, Pete scored forty points a game (in college), and in order to score that much you've got to be an excellent shooter, even though he took a ton of shots. Yeah, Pete was a volume scorer, but he could make ten or fifteen shots in a row on you, too, and go on a run and be dominant. People forget that at times,

Pete was a dominant player on the floor. He could shoot free throws. He was a complete offensive player. In the pros, we used to sag on defense, take lanes away, and beat people up, so it was that much harder to do what he did. Every time he came around me, it was just bang, doing whatever I could to slow him down and wear him down. Maybe you wouldn't win the first quarter, but you try to win the fourth. I just really enjoyed playing against him.

Now with the game being so wide open, and with the three-point shot, to boot, he would be even more dominant. With his size at six-five, and with his long arms and ability to jump—you know he had all that going for him—I think he would be even more dominant. When you look at a player, you have to look at the total package.

Defenses are better now, and that would take some of the stuff away, but the league is trying to allow the offense to flourish more. The way Pete handled the ball, it would really be difficult for a guy like (Allen) Iverson when getting double-teamed, but it would be difficult doing that with Pete because he could go anywhere with a basketball. You couldn't stop him. He could spin on you, go behind his back, he could hesitate, he had a pull-up jumper, he could go all the way to the basket, he had a hook shot, flip shots, he loved to find people—he could do anything with a basketball time and time again, and in different situations. Plus, he could shoot the hell out of it. Right now, what guards can really do all that stuff in a game day in and day out, and with a flair, too, and get people up out of their seats? That's how I remember Pete Maravich.

※※※

JACK MCCALLUM covered the NBA regularly for Sports Illustrated for many years starting in the mid-eighties, and he singles out four players—Larry Bird, Magic Johnson, Isaiah Thomas, and Michael Jordan— as the four players who, to him, defined the NBA during the years he was covering the league. Maravich had retired by the time McCallum started covering the NBA beat for SI in 1985, but the writer had seen enough of Maravich during his playing days to understand his unique brand of greatness and his place in basketball history:

I honestly think that in all the years I covered the NBA that Pete Maravich is the last guy I can remember there being a palpable excitement whenever he touched the ball, and I include Michael Jordan in that. Jordan might have been thirty times better than Maravich as a player, but he didn't inspire me the way Pete did. When it came to finishing a shot, Jordan was perhaps the most exciting ever, like when he would wedge his way in going to the basket. The excitement with Maravich came as soon as he got the ball out on the floor, like when he would get the ball twenty-five feet from the basket and when he started moving his arms all over to fake a pass or whatever, you knew there might be something coming that you had never seen before. He was from the Bob Cousy ancestry of basketball players, although Cousy was slow motion compared to Pete, where Pete was more herky-jerky in how he did things.

Pete was unprecedented in the history of conventional basketball in terms of raising the level of excitement. No one could match him. He had a big part in helping to redefine basketball during that era, forcing such issues as whether it was just a sideshow or a conventional sport, and the idea of ego versus team play. And here he was a white player doing all this at a time when you had all these racial considerations. Yeah, he was a singular character in basketball. But having said all that, he probably wouldn't have been the one guy I would have picked to start a team with. He was just too unpredictable. Compare him to someone like Magic Johnson, who could dump the ball down to Kareem Abdul-Jabbar thirty times a game. Maravich couldn't do that. He would have to do something else. I wouldn't rate Pete as one of the thirty greatest professional basketball players of all time, but he certainly was one of the ten best collegiate players. Yet he was an amazingly star-crossed athlete.

❈

BOB COUSY, *the great and creative point guard of the Boston Celtics dynasty in the fifties and early sixties, has kept close tabs on basketball in the decades since he played, and he credits Maravich as a genuine pioneer in the game:*

I think we both were ahead of our time in terms of what we were able to do when we did it. I was a bit more fortunate because in the last six or seven years of my career, we got our strength and won championships. That allowed me even more freedom to focus on creativity, imagination, and things you'd like to do. Of all the point guards that have played up to now, Pete might have been the most skilled with all the unorthodox things that he could do. But unfortunately, he was neutralized by the fact that he was always with teams where he had to post X number of points. This is contradictory, frankly, to what a point guard's mentality should be going into a game or setting up a play each time. You've got to be coming down, literally, 90 percent of the time looking to create an opportunity for one of the other four people. If the shot clock is winding down and you're out of options, then it's a matter of having the skills to create an opportunity for yourself as a last option, and Pete certainly had them. I don't know if he was ever able to go into a game or situation with that kind of mindset. I think he always went into a game thinking that in order to have a shot at winning, he needed to post at least thirty points. There's no question in my mind, that has to limit your options and creativity. He wasn't able to completely exploit those wonderful, God-given gifts of his.

※※※

For all the things he could do with a basketball in his hands, Maravich could only do what he did with a sort of sixth sense relative to court awareness. CBS college basketball commentator **BILLY PACKER** *has seen a lot of great talent over the years, and what Maravich could do in all facets of the game truly impressed him:*

With his having dexterity with both hands and having the repertoire that he had, the ball was merely an extension of his hands. He never really had to worry about the handle, so consequently not only did he have great vision and awareness, he was also able to make plays in his mind. He not only had the peripheral vision, he also had great knowledge of the game. His father won't go down as one of the coaching legends of all time, but Press had one of the most astute basketball minds that ever participated on the college level. There are certain guys that have great basketball minds that might not have been able to translate that into wins, and Press would be one of those. He was one of those never-ending guys in discussing the game of basketball. Probably his closest friend and ally in the coaching profession was John Wooden, and they were so different from each other in terms of personality. One of the reasons they were so close was that Coach Wooden so respected Press's basketball knowledge and his instinctive nature as to how the game should be played.

Pete, in addition to all the skills that he had, also had the brilliance in the understanding of the game. So now you've got a guy coming down the court on a fast break that has total knowledge of the game, the defense, the offense, where people are to be positioned, how they get there—and in addition to that he has the physical ability in size, speed, and quickness; and then he has this incredible hand-to-eye coordination, and with his hand being an extension of the ball, and then on top of that he has some of the flair that only some of the great Globetrotters or Cousy had. Add all those things together, and there is no one in the history of the game that possesses all of those things better than Pete did.

⊗⊗⊗

Maravich didn't need an arena full of fans to bring out Showtime, as longtime Raleigh, North Carolina, buddy **BOB SANDFORD** *remembers:*

The story I remember the most was when we went to Daytona Beach during the summer one year when he was still at LSU. We were going down the boardwalk one night, a pretty night, and we ran into one of these guys who had a basketball stand set up, like one of those you see at the fair. It was a wooden structure with a net where the ball goes through and rolls back to you. The guy has got these teddy bears and is sitting there without a customer. So Pete goes over and says, "What's going on here? What do you have to do?" The guy says, "For fifty cents if you make two shots you get one of these small teddy bears, or for a dollar you get one of these big teddy bears for making two in a row." So Pete says he wants to try it, and they've got these old rubber balls. Pete picks up one ball and feels around it a little bit. Misses the first one. Picks up the second ball, shoots it, and makes it. He then asks the guy if he can try again. "I want to try for one of those big ones this time." So he gives the guy a dollar. Pete picks up the ball he likes and, boom, he hits it; *boom*, he hits it. Pete says, "I won!" He picks up this big teddy bear and hands it to me, then turns to the guy and says, "I want to try it again." So he picks up the same ball, what he now called his lucky ball, and *bam . . . bam*, he hits two more and says, "I'll take that teddy bear right there." By this time people on the boardwalk are starting to gather around, twenty or twenty-five of them. So Pete hands him another dollar—*bam . . . bam*. Two more in a row. So we eventually got three of these huge teddy bears. He says, "I want to try it again," and the guy says, "No, no, buddy, that's it." And Pete says, "What do you mean?" and by this time there must be fifty people there. Pete's talking loud.

Well, with this structure, there's this wooden board over the top of your head. You're shooting under the board. So Pete says, "Tell you what . . . ," and he backs the crowd way back, and there's a wind blowing out on the beach and he says to the guy, "How about if I shoot from back here?" meaning he had to shoot well beyond what would be a three-point line. And Pete says, "How about I make two more from way back here, do I get another teddy bear?" and the guy says, "Sure." So Pete gives him the dollar and the guy throws him the ball, and this time when Pete caught it, he started spinning it on his finger, off his elbows, and around his head, and people are going crazy. He takes two or three dribbles and *bam*, first shot he knocks the bottom out of it. Second time he gets the ball . . . *bam!* Knocks the bottom out of it again. Now he's made eight shots in a row. The guy said, "That's it. You ain't shootin' any more, buddy." So he took those four teddy bears and gave them to some kids in the crowd. And as we walked off, you could hear people talking about him like he was the Lone Ranger. "Who is that guy?" After a while we told them who it was, and you could hear them saying, "That's Pistol Pete! That's Pistol Pete!" Can't script it any better than that.

⚬⚬⚬

Maravich's flair in passing the ball to open teammates would have made him an extraordinary player on its own, and even many of his teammates in the NBA were stunned by what he could do with the ball, often putting optical illusions to work on his behalf, as former

*Jazz teammate **JIM BARNETT** witnessed at least several times a day or in a game:*

He was ahead of his time. These people who compare Jason Williams to him? He couldn't hold a candle to Pete Maravich! First of all, Pete didn't travel when he made the moves, like Jason does. And no way Jason could shoot like that. You're comparing apples and oranges. In our day, we had to dribble with the hand on top of the ball. When Pete was coming down on the fast break, at any given moment the ball would be out in front of him like it was suspended in air, and he would make a swipe at it with his right hand as though he was going to pass it to his left, but would go underneath the ball and then twist his right hand back over so it was facing back to the right and pass the ball that way to the guy on the right wing, and he did it so smoothly and quick. He was a lot of fun.

⚞⚟

***BOB ROBERTS** was the head coach at Clemson all three years Maravich was playing varsity ball at LSU, and they were friends from way back, with Roberts having been Press Maravich's assistant coach for several years at Clemson. When Clemson played LSU, Maravich always had something up his sleeve, and all Roberts could do sometimes was stare:*

How did we play Pete? I prayed a lot. First time we played them down at LSU, I hadn't seen Pete in four or five years. The players were out in pregame warm-ups and Pete comes down to in front of our bench, and he's doing all this stuff, like taking it between his legs and behind his back, showboating a little bit. And I said, "Pete, have you got a jump shot now?" When he was a kid, you see, he was so weak that he had to bring it from way down and shoot it. Shot it from the hip. He looked me right in the eye and says, "Yeah, Coach, I got me a jump shot and I'm going to show it to you when the game starts." And he did. He fouled out with about five minutes left in the game (having scored thirty-three points). They threw garbage and everything on the floor, and it took them about ten minutes to get the floor cleared.

We were staying in this motel—and they had ended up winning—and we get back to the motel where they're showing the game on tape delay. I walk in and the game is on. The guy at the front desk is sitting there watching the game. Then Pete fouls out. And when he does, the guy running the motel says to the TV, "What do you mean, Pete fouls out?" And I said, "Well, that's five fouls and that's all you get. He's not playing anymore." The guy walks over and turns the television off and says, "If Pete don't play, I'm not watching it." And that was the end of that.

※

*After leaving Tennessee where he had played SEC ball against Maravich, **BILL JUSTUS** went to work for Converse selling basketball shoes, a job that took him throughout the South, giving him ample opportunity to continue seeing Maravich in action:*

I got to see him hit sixty one night and it was very special. It was the circus coming to town. He was one of the top people who had an influence on the game, although people would criticize him because he never played on a championship team. Maybe it was his style of play that prevented his team from being a championship team. As a peer of his, I was also a fan, and it was very unusual to hold a player you play against in such stature. I gawked at what he did, and so did everybody else. I don't know any other way to say this, but the guys who could do these very athletic things, as was the case with many of the black players, they would also stop to watch him play. He would get their attention. But he never played with a winner, so he never got the applause he should have. He still would have fit in at UCLA or anyplace else. But he wouldn't have been who he was if he had gone to a place like that.

Instead, he had a license to do anything that he wanted to at LSU. Any of the rest of us could have been given that same license and we would have failed miserably. James Bond has the license to kill, Pete had the license to thrill—the license to shoot, a license to make any kind of pass that he could create, and he could do it. I could have been told, "Billy, you can do whatever you want to do," and I would have shot four for sixty and thrown the ball away a bunch of times. He was the best I ever saw or played against. From a skills standpoint, nobody was any better. The thing people might not remember is that he had very good lift—he got up well on his jump shot. He was great at freeing himself, but he could also jump over you and shoot it in. He was strong enough to be able to get off those shots from beyond what is now three-point range.

⸎

What if Maravich had been the beneficiary of a three-point line during his three years in the SEC, let alone ten more years in the NBA? Maravich never played with a three-point line, an intriguing scenario that **BILLY PACKER** *enjoys contemplating:*

It would have been phenomenal for him. He had incredible range on his shot. This is something people wouldn't be able to comprehend with him, that he was so great with the ball that you had to worry about his penetration first. If he had had the three-point shot, you would have had to pick him up even farther away from the basket. That would have opened up even more penetrating lanes for him. Not only would it have been the number of points that he would have scored with so many of his twos now being threes, it would have been almost impossible to guard him knowing you had to put so much pressure on him so far away from the basket. At the three-point line, with people guarding him in a box and one or some standard form of defense, all you could try to do out there was contain him, trying to get him to move

AP/Wide World Photos

Whenever Tennessee played LSU, it was up to Volunteers guard Bill Justus (among others) to guard Maravich closely, a task much easier said than done. Here, Justus appears to be headed in one direction while Pete takes the low road.

in some direction. He would have been a fifty-point-a-game scorer without question.

Also, keep in mind that his (approximately) 45 percent shooting average was created by his having to take some bad shots in an attempt to keep his team in the game. You would know that he was not a selfish player if you ever saw him play in summer camp games. In fact, his dad probably worried more about his scoring average than he did. On a good team, his shooting percentage would have gone up considerably, and his scoring average would have come down just slightly, because he wouldn't have been in a position to have to take bad shots.

The only other comparable player I can think of offensively—and Pete was not in this guy's caliber defensively—was Oscar Robertson, in terms of productivity. Oscar was a better rebounder because he was stronger and wouldn't have been as diverse on the break as Pete was. Those are the only two guys in the category of offensive repertoire that you could put in the same category.

❦

*While many of Maravich's ballhandling skills came to him via dozens of skills and tricks taught to him by his father, **BOB COUSY** got most of his ballhandling tricks from up his own sleeve:*

Mine were completely instinctive. You know the old cliché, "Necessity is the mother of invention"? The first time I dribbled behind my back, I did it in college. Everyone ran up to me afterward with the same question, "God, how long have you been practicing that play!?" and I had to tell them that I had never practiced it. Thank goodness, like Pete, I had the God-given skills to be able to execute something like that. Basketball, unlike other team sports—football, for instance, where everything has to be programmed and disciplined—is a game of free flow, imagination, and creativity where an option to a play can work better than the play itself.

In my case, that first time I went behind my back, this guy happened to be playing me hard to my right. It was a last-second situation and we were down by one. They called the play for me, and the right side was cleared out for me. I started going to my right and here's this big football player right there, so I just took it behind my back and caught him by surprise—it caught me by surprise, too—I left him standing there. It gave me a full step on him going back to my left and I dribbled in and made a left-handed hook to win the game. It was the first time I had ever done that, and then I built on that as I went along.

My first six years in the league, (Bill) Sharman, (Ed) MacCauley, and I had to be scorers, but then we got the big guy—Bill Russell—and some other players surrounding us, and that gave me the freedom of expression to be a creative point guard. Pete never had that luxury. Because I could focus on my playmaking skills, I was able to decoy myself and set up opportunities for a bunch of great players.

When it came to fulfillment of skills, Pete probably was the best point guard, physically, and he also had the requisite imagination. It was nice to have someone come along who was doing some of the same things I had been doing ten years before. I think all great athletes in whatever sport it is develop their own style, where people come up to you and say, "Gee, doesn't so-and-so remind you of him?" I never saw anyone that reminded me of me, except maybe Ernie DeGregorio, momentarily. I was coaching college at the time and I was scouting him when he was at Providence. It was almost spooky. I would watch him and say to myself, "Now, dip that shoulder and then go right. Move the defender and then make the bounce pass." He would function in that way. In terms of the passing game and how he set things up, I saw some similarities. After that, I didn't see any comparable players.

Likewise, there's never been a player, in my judgment, who ever played like Pete, either. The great ones are unique in how they do something. I think it applies across the board in most sports. Like, there have been a lot of great running backs, but has there ever been another Walter Payton or someone who would remind you of him? I don't think so, except perhaps Gale Sayers. Magic (Johnson) had his own style, and he was imaginative and creative and did it from a six-nine frame, but in terms of creativity, I don't put him in the same class with Maravich or myself.

※※※

*Maravich's "Showtime" reputation was further bolstered by the public and posted accolades that often greeted the Tigers wherever they went, and teammates like **RICH HICKMAN** took notice:*

One time for an away game, and I don't remember where it was, after we got off the plane and took our bus to the hotel, the marquee there said, "Welcome Pistol Pete and Team." So as a prank, before the game, we took our warm-ups and our shooting jackets with our last names on them—Pete's had "Pistol" on it—and we created temporary signs for each of our jackets that said "Team." Press was hot, even though we thought it was a good joke. That was the last time we did that.

※※※

It's an interesting piece of pop-culture history to go back more than thirty years and see how the print media of that era of Aquarius and flowers in our hair treated Maravich in writing:

LSU's Pete Maravich is typical of the age in which we live, the computer age. He is programmed to throw a basketball through a hoop, and for two straight seasons he has done it more often than anybody in college basketball.

And, with six games already behind him this season, the floppy-haired wizard is off to another great start with a 49-point average and his team sporting a 5-1 record.

Who said computers aren't any good?

But Pistol Pete (No. 23) is no computer. He is a member of the young generation. The long, floppy hair; the mod terminology, and an eye for flair.

He is also in demand. Everybody wants to see him, talk to him, or get his autograph on that 50-cent program.[2]

RALPH JUKKOLA *is another of Maravich's LSU*
teammates who associated the word Showtime with
Maravich at the mere mention of the name:

When I think of Pete, I think "Showtime." Most every
game, you'd go out there wondering if he was going to do
something different. There was always a sense of anticipation. One time we were playing Tulane and Pete was hurt—
I think it was his left knee. And Tulane's coach at the time
kept saying, "Make him go left! Make him go left! He can't
go left, he's hurt!" And I think they held him to about sixty
that time. We all knew he could go left okay, and we
thought it was great, because they were letting him go left,
and hell, he could go left or right and shoot just as well
either way. In fact, I think he could even shoot a little better going to his left because, being a right-hander, it's a better bank shot from that angle, and he could certainly bank
shots. After the game their coach said something like,
"Man, if that boy ever played for me, he'd never get on the
court." Well, whoopee ding-dang. Here's a guy scoring
forty or fifty points a game and you're not going to play
him!? Get real.

It wasn't an integral part of the Showtime act, but the
LSU basketball team ended up traveling in their own
airplane, and at times, that was done with a true
Maravich flair, as **DONALD RAY KENNARD** *points out:*

We traveled in a DC-3. We had bought the plane from the
governor of Mississippi. And Press was a pilot. He had
bombed a whale in World War II. He thought it was a sub-
marine surfacing. Back in those days you had those old
phones where you had to go through the operator. Press
would say, "Ma'am, I'd like to call Hartford, Connecticut,"
and they would go, "What's your name?" and he would say,

"Maravich." But they could never get it right. "Well," he would say, "it rhymes with a certain word."

One time we were in Auburn and leaving to play Mississippi State on a Sunday afternoon. We get to Mississippi State and there are three cows on the runway. It's really cold, so rather than being on the cold grass and wet ground, they got onto that concrete. So we circled two or three times. Starkville didn't have an airport tower, just a runway out in the middle of nowhere near campus. After our circling two or three times, the campus police saw what was happening, so they came over and ran the cows off the runway so that we could land. You remember things like that.

The games we would go to, there would be so many writers covering it that Pete usually had a press conference of at least thirty or forty-five minutes. He would always be the last one in the shower and the last one to leave. If you were with the media in, say, Atlanta or Lexington or Knoxville, you had traveled 125 to 200 miles to see the kid play, and that was the only way you could ever interface with him. He was a guy who never met a pencil he didn't like—he would give an autograph to anybody.

What I remember about him is his freshman year. Remember the little 45-rpm records? I would go in his room and his favorite thing was having those 45s stacked up, ten records deep, and drop down one at a time, and he would sit there and study while listening to the music. He had a little lamp on his desk. When you're an academic adviser, as I was, you're their father away from home.

We had a lot of deep conversations. I'd go in there at night, sit on a corner of his bed while he was at his desk, and we'd sit there and talk about whatever was on his mind. He would come over to my office and I'd say, "Pete, the registrar wants to meet you." So naturally, when I took him to see the registrar, he would have a staff of about twenty people and they would all come over to get an autograph. The girls would want a lock of his hair. I took him all around campus, and would say, "Hey, Pete, Mary over in the speech department wants to meet you, and you know you're taking speech this semester." He was a good student and majored in business administration. I think he had a 2.4 (GPA) when he left.

⊗⊗⊗

Longtime LSU sports announcer JOHN FERGUSON *was doing radio play-by-play during the Maravich era and he saw things that years later he would find comparable to another extraordinary basketball superstar:*

The LSU fast break in those years was so far ahead of its time, and I can still get a mental picture of LSU's fast break with Maravich in the middle and two guys coming down on the outside. It was a full-speed thing and, a lot of times, at about the top of the key Maravich would go way up in the air à la Michael Jordan and he would make all kinds of moves in the air. Sometimes it would seem, and just like it was with Michael Jordan, when he got to the apex of his jump he would reach back and get something from somewhere that allowed him to go even higher. And the defensive players didn't know if the ball was going to be coming from between his legs, behind his back, under his arms, and even if he was going to pass it. They just didn't know.

He was a real staunch competitor. One time we played at Alabama before a full arena, and among those people were a lot of Alabama students, including practically all the members of the Alabama football squad. Well, they taunted Maravich, and Maravich taunted them back. This went on the entire game. LSU had a highly productive game and won with a big score. Not much defense going on there. Pete gave them the bird and everything else you can think of. At the end of the game, Maravich took a lap around the place giving them all the bird and so forth, and next thing you know thousands of kids came down on the floor and they had one of the biggest fights of all time in the SEC. He engendered that kind of competitive spirit. Doesn't in any way diminish his influence on the game or what he did during the game, but he was a competitor.

∞

The Crimson Tide coach in those days was **C. M. NEWTON,** *who recently retired as the athletic director at the University of Kentucky. Newton was as awed by Maravich's skills as an opposing coach dared to be, and his strategy in playing LSU was to let Pete get his shots and his forty-plus points a game:*

His sixty-nine-point record was against one of my Alabama teams, in Tuscaloosa and on TV. He was a great player, the most skilled basketball player I've ever been around. Now, I think Michael Jordan was a better player. He had a big effect on basketball in the SEC. Just with my own son, Martin. With the youth program at Alabama, we started something called the Bama Bouncers. We took Pete's training film on ballhandling skills, and actually got with him, and I felt the best way to motivate young basketball players was through ballhandling. Pete had a profound impact on a lot of kids, not just the ones who went around with floppy socks and that kind of stuff, but the ballhandling stuff mainly.

My biggest fear of Pete when coaching against him was that I always thought he was a better passer and set his teammates up better than he actually was a scorer. Yeah, he was scoring his forty-four points a game, but my concern was that he would also get Apple Sanders to score ten and Bill Newton fifteen and some other guy fourteen if we doubled up on him, so we played him head-up. We conceded his average and tried not to let him have the really big night. Other people doubled him, but then he would still get his average and make the other guys better.

∞

Veteran basketball writer **CURRY KIRKPATRICK** *not only considers Maravich one of the game's greatest players but also a central figure to his own love of the game as he once hinted at in a* Sports Illustrated *column paying homage to Maravich soon after the Pistol's death:*

Pistol Pete was special to me. He was the subject of the first cover story I wrote for *Sports Illustrated*—when he was a sophomore at LSU in 1968. More than that, he personified why I love basketball; why I enjoy watching it, writing about it; why sport itself is such an important part of human existence. Simply put, Maravich was terrific fun. In the history of college basketball there have been other marvelously talented players—Wilt, Russ, Elgin, Big O, West, the Bird—but at the top of his game, when he was smoking out another outrageous fifty-point night, absolutely nobody, no time, nowhere approached Maravich. . . . He was Cousy long after Cousy, and Magic even before Magic. An entertainer. The one-and-only. The star.[3]

LOU CARNESECCA, *longtime Saint John's coach, on Maravich following a Rainbow Classic loss to LSU:*

He's always entertaining, he's always on. He dazzles you and electrifies the crowd. I'm supposed to be the coach and I'm supposed to be watching the whole game. I would end up just watching him. He can pass better than Bob Cousy and Dick McGuire, shoot better than Oscar Robertson and has moves he hasn't even tried yet.[4]

LEN WILKENS, *a Hall of Fame guard and legendary NBA coach, on Maravich:*

The problem with Pete was that he was born too soon. People would love him today. But Pete was a little before his time, a bit out of context. People labeled him a hotdog for doing things that are widely accepted today.[5]

∞∞

A verse from the "Ballad of Pete Maravich," by **WOODY JENKINS:**

> Maravich, oh Maravich,
> Love to fake, love to score,
> Love to hear the people roar.
> Just a boy of twenty-two,
> You made a name at LSU,
> You've much more yet to do.[6]

∞∞

LSU football star **TOMMY CASANOVA** *was a big basketball fan during the Maravich era at LSU, and is as quick to tell basketball tales as he is football stories when regaling listeners with memories of his days at LSU:*

There have been great athletes and players who have achieved more, but I don't think I've ever seen anyone else who could do with a basketball what Pete could do. I've seen his arms extend out to the left coming down midcourt on a two-on-two with a guy on his left and looking like he's going to make a pass to the left and his hands go out that way, but the ball bounces back behind him to the right to another guy—Apple Sanders—who catches the ball in midstride and lays it up—and no one even saw this third guy coming down the court.

To this day, I don't know how Pete made that pass, but he did. His shooting and his ballhandling were unbelievable, but his passes were just beyond belief. He was the most entertaining athlete I've ever seen. You never knew what was going to happen next. I got to know the basketball players and through them I knew that their game plan was to be expecting a ball any time no matter where you are on the court because if you're open, Pete is going to hit you.

His dad was just as entertaining and had a marvelous sense of humor. In this one game, and I don't remember who it was against, somebody took one of those giveaway seat cushions and just sailed it out over the crowd like a Frisbee, and it landed on the court. Naturally, when that happens, another one comes down, then another, and all of a sudden five or six are raining down. The officials are having to stop the game to clean these things off the court, and the coaches were up waving and yelling for the fans to stop it.

When the PA announcer makes an announcement for them to stop, well, the more they come. So Press storms over to the microphone, grabs it, and says, "Now listen. We love your support and we love your enthusiasm. I love it. The team loves it. We need it. But quit throwing those damn cushions!" The place went absolutely nuts, but not another seat cushion came flying out. It was a show, just wonderful entertainment, and if Pete couldn't do it, his daddy could.

⊱⊰⊱⊰

What we now refer to as "Showtime" was called other things during the sixties and early seventies, when college basketball, especially in the South, was in an advanced state of infancy, and where dramatic flair and behind-the-back passes were akin to UFO sightings and stereotypes were just starting to be demolished, as the following two excerpts from a 1970 Atlanta Journal and Constitution Magazine *article bear out:*

Newstyle basketball is basically a contribution of the sixties from the black ghettoes of the North. While Oldstyle basketball was oriented to the eye and separated everything into parts (individual stars, X's on the floor, and a mechanistic relationship of parts), the Newstyle basketball was quite different, being oriented more to space, its special sensory

equipment seemingly located mainly in the skin and muscles, and becoming for the first time a truly team sport.
Indeed, Newstyle basketball is organic in the sense that the
ball itself had become the seat of all consciousness, the players becoming its arms and legs and driving force, serving it
with an intense and quite old-fashioned ethos, like that of
the late knight errant who might go through all sorts of
rather beautiful and strange contortions for the favor of one
flashing two-point smile. It's basketball's romantic period.[7]
    . . . And then something happens. Pete Maravich gets the
ball and though a moment before he'd been one with the
complex of feints and thrusts and probings of weak spots,
the squeaks of sneakers, and the waving arms, now with the
ball he's full of a non-discursive meaning. And—ah!—a
lurid meaning it is, if you note it carefully, for the ball is no
longer a center of consciousness in the hands of Pete
Maravich; it's an appendage of some sort, an extension of the
Pete Maravich will, if you please; and more, obviously, for on
his face, usually so placid and glazed-over, now is the awful
look of an animal need. Pete Maravich is full of lust. And
we're fascinated by it, for somewhere in this near-indecent
exposure stirs the recognition that we're entering the age of
basketball sex.[8]

*The Maravich brand of Showtime was squelched
somewhat during his turbulent days playing for the
Atlanta Hawks, as teammate JIM WASHINGTON
explains:*

Pete was a very flamboyant kind of player, very flashy. If you
compared him to today's talent, he would fit in very well. I
see this kid playing today for Sacramento, Jason Williams,
and the resemblance is uncanny, the style of play. But we
were not successful as a team, and I think Pete internalized
that a lot. I think he felt it was up to him to help us win the
conference championship and to be a real strong contender

for the title, but that did not materialize and he did not accept that very well.

Unfortunately, he felt a lot of pressure and responsibility to do it, and that reflected in his game. He was not one of those guys who was able to blend his talents into a team effort. He thought it rested on his shoulders to do all the things necessary, when in fact we had other players who were very capable to assist him in reaching that accomplishment.

∞∞

Former Auburn star **JOHN MENGELT** *draws on thirty years of elapsed basketball history in trying to put some perspective on what Maravich brought to the game in terms of flair and entertainment:*

Opposing fans didn't like him, but I guess opposing fans didn't like me, and if they didn't like me, that made me feel kind of good about it. On the road, boos were like cheers. But Pete had the long hair and floppy socks, and handled the ball in such a way that he was an anomaly to a lot of people. It was show-offy to them and they thought it was a ploy on his part to embarrass the other team, but it was just part of his game. It just made him feel more comfortable playing that way, and it turned him up as well as turned up his team-mates. I don't think he was trying to show off. It was just a part of a game, but still, a lot of people didn't like that. So there was probably a little more animosity toward him than toward somebody else like me.

My being from Indiana, there were a lot of guys who could handle a ball like that. They taught us at age three or four to put the ball into our left hand, to become ambidextrous in handling it. To me I don't know that I had seen that level of showmanship, but I had seen guys in high school who could dribble between their legs and pass the ball behind their backs. But I had never seen anyone do it with the flair that he did it. Some guys who played against him got caught up in watching him, and I never let that happen.

That's dangerous. I did some of that in the pros. Third game in my career I'm standing next to Elgin Baylor and Jerry West and Wilt's there, too, and I was in awe playing them.

⚘

MARAVICH, *on his flashy style of play:*

I play like I practice. The flashy things are the natural way to me, and that's why I do the things the way I do.[9]

⚘

MARAVICH, *on the beauty of a good pass versus a great shot:*

When we are playing at home, I can make a good pass and you can't even hear yourself think. The fans know you can shoot; the pass gives them something extra. It is entertainment.[10]

5

FULLCOURT PRESS

No story or book about Pete Maravich is, or can be, complete without more than a token reference to his dad, Peter "Press" Maravich. Theirs wasn't always a smooth father-son relationship, but it was a potent one. Press was the ultimate Little League dad—a walking encyclopedia of chalk talks and understanding of the game's intricacies with a willingness to teach Pete everything he knew while motivating his son to new heights. There have been other prodigal athletic sons over the years—quarterback Todd Marinovich and golfer Tiger Woods come to mind—but neither had the benefit of a dad who knew as much about their son's sport as Press Maravich. And that's with apologies to Earl Woods.

Starting from the time his son could barely walk, Press was putting a basketball into young Pete's hands and pointing toward the basketball goal in the backyard. Not that Pete needed a map or compass to find his way, but he had a father who not only knew how to get there, he knew what to do with the ball once he got within sight of a basketball net. One popular take on Press and Pete at LSU is that Press must have gotten hired as some sort of package deal to get Pete to follow in his dad's footsteps to LSU. There may or may not be some or a lot of truth to that, but to imply that Press got a free ride because of his son is to not know basketball. Fathers have gotten hired as token college assistants to get their blue-chip sons to follow suit, but remember that Press was hired as head coach and had already had ample experience as a Division I head coach, most recently at Clemson and then North Carolina State. Not long before taking the LSU job, Press had coached an undermanned Wolfpack team to the championship of the prestigious, battle-scarred Atlantic Coast Conference. It had been an N.C. State from which no starter would go on to gain a foothold in the NBA.

Four years together as father and son, coach and player, weren't always easy for Press and Pete Maravich at LSU. There was the occasional and mutual sniping during practices and games, and Press's less-than-loving way of criticizing Pete to his face and saving the praises, like for one of Pete's creative dribbles, for behind Pete's back. Press Maravich was a lifelong basketball savant, soaking up basketball knowledge and then dispensing his distilled version of what he had learned to his players, most noticeably Pete. Theirs was an up-and-down relationship, although both came to terms with life and each other in the mid-eighties while Press was slowly and agonizingly dying from cancer, ultimately achieving victory with his son by joining him in a profession of dedication to Jesus Christ not long before he passed away—with Pete to follow less than a year later. Again, in his daddy's footsteps.

≈≈≈≈

JOHN WOODEN was arguably the greatest college basketball coach who ever lived and perhaps his profession's most stoic, distinguished legend, but he was close friends with Press Maravich—a complete

personality opposite—and that was in part because of
his respect for Press's knowledge of the game, which
had been on display during the many summers when
they coached together at the Campbell College
basketball camp in North Carolina:

I had a lot of discussions with Press over the years. He
would say that Pete was going to become the first millionaire
pro player and I would say, "But will he play on a championship team?" I remember watching Pete when he was in
junior high, and even then he could do more things with a
basketball than I had ever seen anyone do, and that includes
the Harlem Globetrotters. I also thought he would have been
better off learning more about playing defense. As for Press,
I don't think there has ever been a coach who knew basketball better than he did. There were times in my coaching
career when I would encounter some kind of problem and
then call him, and I would always get something positive
from him. I don't know if he was a great teacher of the game
in terms of getting the most out of his teams, but he certainly understood the game as well as anybody.

※

CBS commentator BILLY PACKER also was a veteran
of the Campbell College summer camp, where he got
the chance to tap into basketball intellects the likes of
Press Maravich and John Wooden:

Press was a coach who had very few enemies. My coach was
Bones McKinney, and Bones and Press were very close
friends. It was a different day, a different era where there
were these incredible personal relationships even though
they were also competitors. My father also was a college
coach and I would put him in the same category as a Press
Maravich because they were guys who loved to study things
and talk about the game. So I had a bonding with Press that
was kind of special, even though he was an adversary.

He was a guy with a great sense of humor. He was a competitor even though he didn't have a great record at Clemson, but he did have a pretty good record at N.C. State and did okay at LSU compared to what had happened there before. He had great compassion for his son, and this was not an ego trip to have his son being the leading scorer in the nation because he worked Petey harder as a kid than about any father I had seen, yet there was a great bonding between the two. Press liked to coach, he liked to teach, he liked to push, and Pete loved to listen, to learn, and to be pushed. So it was probably the greatest father-and-son basketball combination in the history of the sport, and it was one of great mutual respect and kinship.

⊱⊰

Fellow television basketball analyst **DICK VITALE** *remembers Press Maravich for his passion and exuberance for the game of basketball and for Pete's involvement in the game:*

I remember him putting on clinics, being a young coach myself and going to clinics to learn as much as I can. His eyes used to light up like you can't believe when he talked about his son. It's very difficult in this day and age to coach your own kid, to be able to deal with that kind of situation unless your son is clearly, clearly, the best, and there was no question about that with the Pistol. We would always get so enthralled about the guy's skills and ability, but people have no idea what is involved to get there. You just can't go on the floor and do what he did without having someone guiding you and directing you and supervising you as you're doing the drills, and then having the unbelievable willpower to put those drills into force every day for hours and hours. That's what his dad used to do.

There's no shortcut, man. It's perspiration. There's a saying that says, "Genius is 1 percent inspiration and 99 percent perspiration." And I think that reflects Pistol Maravich. He was a genius with a basketball in his hands because he perspired like hell every day, in the sun, hours and hours when other guys were going to the beach or out partying—his party was his dream, his ball, and his goals.

⤬

Press Maravich dearly loved his son and loved teaching him new skills to practice, but it wasn't all lovey-dovey between father and son as LSU student DANNY YOUNG, who traveled with the team to perform sports information duties, quickly learned over the years:

Press was real hard on Pete. He drove him and was constantly complaining about this or that, saying, "You can do this better." And I think Pete tried like hell to please Press, and certainly Press was very pleased and proud, but he didn't show it to Pete that much. Most of the time when Press "put the hat" on Pete, he came through; he either won the game or something happened and he got fouled. Then, of course, there were the drills he went through before the game.

For the freshman games at least, they would do the "Sweet Georgia Brown" theme and he would perform, and everybody came to watch the routine. Even the other players tried to get into it, behind the back and through the legs. But Pete would spin the ball, around, over, and behind his head, just doing all kinds of things. Press would go from hot to cold watching this. You never knew how Press was going to come out. He would get on Pete something fierce like, "Damn, you can't miss those kinds of shots," or "You gotta do this or gotta do that." Then he would turn around and tell someone else, "Man, they fouled the (crap) out of him (Pete)," although he wouldn't tell him that. Yet he was always complimenting Pete to everyone else.

⤬

As much as he worked with Pete Maravich in his role
as LSU sports information director, **BUD JOHNSON**
said he knew, and enjoyed, Press better as a person:

Press was a lot more interesting than Pete because when I
first met Pete he was just a young, immature kid, albeit one
with a lot of talent. What do you talk to a seventeen-year-old
about anyway? Not much for very long. But Press was very
interesting. He was a coach who read books, for one thing,
and I thought that was interesting. One day they were going
over into Israel, a combat zone, and Press and Pete were
going over there to put on a clinic. He found out about the
terrorism, about people putting bombs in vehicles, and stuff
like that. They had this driver who would pick them up
every morning, and Press would wait until this guy had
started the car before he'd get in. He'd say, "Pete, let's wait
until they start the car."

   Press always had good relations with the sports information department. But I don't think he was trying to get any
more ink for his son simply because there really wasn't any
way for Pete to get any more ink than he did. Press gave me
a lot of good advice as a young SID. There were some guys in
Baton Rouge who were not really into basketball. I would
mumble and grumble about that, and Press said, "Hey, you
got a national commodity, LSU football, and pretty soon
you're going to have a national commodity in Pete," and he
told me that even before I saw Pete play. And he wasn't arrogant in how he said it.

❧

Former LSU play-by-play announcer **JOHN FERGUSON**
describes Press's concern for his son's basketball career
as an obsession:

Press was obsessed with his son and the game. He knew
his boy was a great player. They came to LSU as a package.
I don't think there was any question about that. (LSU's

then-athletic director) Jim Corbett was the man who recruited the coach to get the son. Press was a guy who recognized what he had in his son, and he built his coaching career around him. He was successful, but I think he was obsessed by the fact his son was a great player. He wore out all of the film made at that time of this great player. I suspect you can't find a foot of film anywhere that isn't worn out, or with scratches because it's been run and run and rerun thousands of times. It was not uncommon for the coach, the father, to be away for days at a time studying this stuff, marveling at it really. He was a man who really knew the game, although he had family problems up to here, and those had to weigh heavily on him. When Pete went on to the NBA, it was only a matter of time (at LSU) for Press, because now his star was gone.

❦

GREG BERNBROCK *was Pete's freshman coach, putting him into position to become a Press Maravich disciple:*

Press Maravich took a keen interest in his coaches, players, and team. I had already lost my dad, and like lots of fathers and sons, we were tight and he taught me a lot about basketball. Press then came along and filled the void as a "father figure" and true friend. We spent hours together, along with Coach (Jay) McCreary, working on strategies, recruiting, watching film, and preparing for opponents. All of this was very enjoyable work. Many nights after practice he would invite me over for ham sandwiches and Cokes, and we'd talk more basketball, often till the wee hours of the morning. I used to get him to laugh a lot, too, which was really important because he was under more pressure than the average head coach, coaching his son with monumental expectations.

Press forgot more about basketball than a lot of coaches will ever know. He was very close to John Wooden, the

LSU SPORTS INFORMATION DEPARTMENT PHOTO

All things considered, Press Maravich, like most coaching dads, probably cared more about his son's play than that of any of his other players, but he was a coach highly regarded by his peers nonetheless.

famous UCLA coach, and they roomed together each summer at Campbell College in North Carolina. Prior to coming to LSU, Press was handpicked by Everett Case, the great North Carolina State coach, to succeed him as N.C. State's head coach. He had two great seasons at N.C. State, going something like 49-12, prior to coming to LSU. A lot of pro coaches thought very highly of Press, including Red Auerbach, the leader of the world-champion Boston Celtics.

I remember that Jerry Colangelo of the Phoenix Suns was a friend, and there were always rumors that Press would eventually be handed either an NBA or ABA job.

Press had a quick wit and loved the game of basketball. One night I picked him up in Lexington and drove him into eastern Kentucky to see Pat Tallent, a highly recruited high school player who played in a high school gym that couldn't have been any wider than six or seven bowling alleys laid next to each other. Anyway, the minute Pat got his hands on the ball, he was a threat. He scored something like fifty points. After the game, I took Press over to meet Pat's mom, who was tallying up his points. Press winked at her, and she immediately recognized him as the famous LSU coach. Press wanted to know how many points Pat had scored, and Ms. Tallent had every one of them right there on her scorecard. It was funny seeing Press and Ms. Tallent counting point by point all the baskets that Pat had made. Press was a very meticulous person, and this was his way of spending quality time with a recruit's mother, even though hordes of people were standing all around him.

Press was very much ahead of his time, which is one reason why Pete was such an incredible talent, even at an early age. Every great talent I've ever known, be it in sports or business or whatever, had a tremendous amount of natural ability. We often refer to these gifted individuals as "unconscious competents." In other words, they seem to know instinctively what to do at a given time, especially in the heat of battle.

One time we were playing fourth-ranked Duquesne for the championship of the All-College Tourney. We got the ball out of bounds underneath our basket with one second left on the clock and needing a basket to win. We huddled to plan the win, and Press diagrammed a surprise play that we had discussed earlier in the week preparing for the tournament. We had never practiced this play. It was gut instinct by a great coach. We had our big three frontliners form a wall and had Pete tuck in right behind them. When our guard taking the ball out yelled "Hit it!" all three frontliners fell straight to the floor and every Duquesne player looked down in surprise. We threw the ball to Pete for a lay-up quicker than you could say your name and it was over, just that fast! But Press had that type of feel for the game and, yes, it helps to have been a successful college and pro player, which Press had been.

❧

Press Maravich was gruff and could rub people the wrong way with his abrasive language, but as New Orleans Times-Picayune *sportswriter* **MARTY MULE** *learned over time, once you got beyond that hard wall, Press turned out to be a good coach and a pretty good guy:*

Press was a very generous guy, a fun guy to be around. Pete could be funny, but it was a kind of wry, tongue-in-cheek sense of humor, Press was a back slapper, a jokester so to speak. He was very good offensively. You can't use his record at LSU as a gauge because he was building a program. One of those years, I think it was Pete's junior or senior year, LSU was like second or third in the nation in scoring and he was finally putting the pieces together. It was offset a little because they weren't a great defensive team, but he was an excellent offensive coach.

❧

MARAVICH, *on the "fireside chalk talks" that took place at the Maravich house during Press's coaching days at Clemson University:*

My mom always brewed fresh hot coffee for Dad and his coaching buddies in anticipation of the late nights of basketball rhetoric. He had a wealth of knowledge to draw on, and like a wise old sage he was willing to talk with anyone who wanted to knock around new ideas or reminisce about old ones. Late-night discussions were especially formative times for me.[1]

✂

Former Alabama basketball coach and all-around SEC legend **C. M. NEWTON** *was among dozens of coaches who knew both Press and Pete well:*

I was a big fan of both Press and Pete. He was a respectful, almost shy kind of young man very interested in basketball and he wanted to help others with basketball. Press was a gruff, no-nonsense kind of guy, yet he was fun-loving in a lot of ways. He was a heck of a basketball coach, and a very good teacher. He was not a good recruiter. He never had great talent other than Pete, and he didn't recruit Pete; he fathered him. He was the old-type, solid basketball guy who loved the game and loved discipline.

✂

TOMMY HESS, *one of Pete's LSU teammates, hoped to eventually join Press Maravich on his coaching staff, but those plans never came to fruition:*

The plays Press set up were incredible, and the only other person I knew as good as that at the collegiate level was Lou Carnesecca, because he was good at setting up box and ones for his people like Chris Mullins. And Press was one of the greatest. A lot of the plays that I used when I was coaching high school basketball I got from Press on getting your star player open on fades and curls and stuff like that. He probably initiated stuff that a lot of coaches use now.

When I was at LSU, my goal was to coach college basketball after I got out of LSU, and Press was going to hire me. But in April of my senior year, Press got fired by LSU. I can still remember that day. I hadn't heard about it when I went to see him in his office, and when I walked in I saw him sitting there with his feet propped up on the desk. Jay

McCreary was sitting over in a corner with tears in his eyes and Greg Bernbrock was biting his fingernails. I knew right away there was a problem because sometime earlier Press had given up stogies and cussing, and when I went in there I saw that he had a cigar in his hand. Then when I asked what was wrong, he said, "Those mother—— fired me!"

I saw my life flash before my eyes in terms of becoming a college coach. He said I could go to Appalachian State with him, but I decided not to. To this day, I believe Papa Press and two other coaches, Tex Winter and Vic Bubas, initiated what became known as the triangle offense—the one that Michael Jordan was a part of while playing with the Chicago Bulls. I think those three came up with the offense while sitting around at a basketball camp in Pennsylvania. I used to love sitting around listening to those guys talk basketball.

⋙⋘

*LSU forward **DANNY HESTER** saw Press Maravich as a player's kind of coach, as he explains:*

Press was a great guy, a player's coach. The way he approached the game—and, of course, he had Pete along with everything else—was to outscore everyone else, and, if you did, you win. Second, we didn't focus on defense and we were an offense-oriented team, and Pete was the one who spearheaded that whole thing. Get the ball and run.

We were scoring more points than about anyone back in those days. They didn't have the thirty-second clock in yet, so a lot of teams would try to stall the ball—North Carolina with the four corners—teams would try to sit on the ball with Pete, but as soon as we got our hands on the ball we were off and running again. Bottom line, it was fun to play for Press, and he was fun to play with. He knew a lot about the game, but his approach was to get out there and have fun.

⋙⋘

It's not easy being a "players' coach," walking the tightrope between being a disciplinarian and a player's friend, and yet LES ROBINSON, a former player and assistant coach under Press, claims that Maravich came about as close to pulling it off as anyone could:

Press had a great relationship with players. He was the one coach I had who could be close to the players and yet he was tough as hell. He had a great relationship and I just liked that. When he was an assistant coach, he would chew your butt out, but at the end of practice he would put his arm around players and encourage them.

When I became freshman coach (at N.C. State), I realize now, looking back, he put a lot more confidence in me than I could have put in a young man twenty-two years old. Scouting. Recruiting. I didn't know anything about finances or house payments and he would share information about everything. He was a unique character that had a huge heart and had great compassion for people, to a fault. That year that I was the freshman coach, there were a lot of things I learned that I didn't know that I had learned until about four or five years down the road.

At Coach Maravich's funeral (in April 1986), my wife and I were standing up at the casket and Pete hugged me. When Coach Maravich died, he died quietly. Many people didn't know about his death. The funeral was going to be on Good Friday. I called Russ Bergman—the only guy other than me who both played and coached under Coach Maravich—because I knew how close he was to Press. As fate would have it, I was in east Tennessee and I tracked Russ down; he was with his wife in the mountains of North Carolina just twenty-five minutes from me.

We got into a car that afternoon and drove until three o'clock in the morning to get to Pittsburgh for the funeral the next morning. I was the only person there from the '65 ACC championship team, even though I had been a coach that season. Pete came over to me and said something to the effect that "your team was my dad's favorite of all-time." He had tears in his eyes as he hugged me, and then he said, "It was his favorite team and because it was his favorite, it was my favorite team, too." The reason was that we were such overachievers.

⚛️

OLIN BROADWAY, *Pete's first head coach at Needham-Broughton High School in Raleigh, knew Press Maravich as more than just the coaching father of the new kid in town:*

I knew him before, when he was coaching at Clemson and I was playing at Wake. Bones (McKinney) was a pretty good friend of Press's, and Bones carried me around more than he did some of the other players because I was his captain. So I knew Press through a lot of that, things like Campbell College. Press was a very interesting guy. If he were losing, he would often say, "I should have stayed in Aliquippa and become a foreman in the steel mill." He thought maybe he could have made more money doing that, and I think he was kidding. I liked Press a lot. He was supportive of what we did in the school and he was supportive of Pete. He and Pete had a very interesting relationship. They carried on with each other a good bit. Press would come into the gym, usually after practice to pick Pete up, saying it's time to go home for dinner. But Pete would say something like, "But I haven't finished my foul shooting yet." And Press would look at me and say, "How do you like that kid?"

⚛️

RICH HICKMAN *was another of Pete's LSU teammates who was enamored of Press Maravich— some of the time:*

In certain ways he was very demanding, and in certain other ways he was lax. There were some things he'd let Pete get away with that he really couldn't come down on us for doing the same stuff. So got himself between a rock and a hard spot in that regard. He was the kind of guy who would yell and scream and cuss at the drop of a hat, whether it was practice, a game, or when we went over to the house to visit.

He didn't want any of the guys dating. He thought women were the ruination of athletes. When he found out we were dating somebody, he would say, "What in the hell are you doing?" And we'd say, "Don't worry, Coach. Got it covered, got it covered." He wanted you to think basketball all day long all year long. And anything that distracted from that was not good. I'd take what he said with a grain of salt and then go off and do my thing. He made it a point to keep up with us to make sure we were keeping our grades up, but sometimes he would say, "Don't let the classwork get in the way of basketball, but do enough to stay in school."

⚬⚬⚬

*During his days as an assistant coach under Press at N.C. State, **LES ROBINSON** would often team up with Pete—who was still in high school—to put basketball recruits through a playing test while Press waited back in his office for the expert assessments:*

From a recruiting standpoint, they didn't have all those blue-chip ratings and networking around the country, so we didn't know if a guy coming up in Indiana or California or wherever was really any good or not. So when we got a recruit in, Coach Maravich would have me take them over to the gym across the street. We would bring two guys in, and Pete and I would play these kids two on two. We would beat them like three or four straight times and it was like a joke. Then I would go back to Coach Maravich and give him my assessment of the kid. Well, this one kid I told Coach Maravich about, I said, "Coach, I just don't think he can cut it in the ACC." My standard of evaluation was how a guy would play against Pete, and I knew Pete was very, very good, but I misjudged just how good he was in terms of comparing him to these recruits. This one guy we turned down went on to make all–Big Ten. I did it with some other players who went on to have good college careers. My bar was so high because I was comparing them to Pete. I mean, these kids were going against the fastest gun in the West, and there's only one fastest gun, and we didn't know until later that Pete was the fastest gun.

⨯⨯

BOB ROBERTS *was Press Maravich's first assistant-coach hire at Clemson, and it was an opportunity that Roberts never forgot to appreciate:*

He worked there by himself the first couple of years. I ended up going over there and worked for him for four of the greatest years of my life. Press was a unique individual. Basketball was this guy's life—that's all he thought about it. His basketball knowledge in the time we were together was as good as anyone's could ever have been. He knew what everyone did, and I don't think there was a coach who knew more about the X's and O's of the game. We didn't have the talent, but he knew exactly what the other team was going to do whenever we played somebody. He was unbelievable.

We wanted to play man-to-man, but he said, "We've got to come up with an offense that we can play against any defense regardless of what it is." And I said, "Whatever you think." He said, "Just think about it and we'll work on it." We got all that worked out, and then he said, "Okay, now we've got to come up with a name for it. So think about it." About three or four days later, I walk into his office one morning at about eight o'clock and he's jumping up and down, and says, "I've got it! A name for our offense." And I said, "Well, what is it?" And he said, "Junto. J-U-N-T-O." I said, "Junto? I like the name but—" And he said, "Just listen. J is for joined. U-N—united. T-O—together." Later on after he left Clemson to coach at N.C. State—and by then I was head coach at Clemson—we're playing them, and he jumps up and starts hollering, "Junto!!" And I looked over and started laughing, and said, "Hey, Press, I know what you're doing."

Getting back to when Press first got to Clemson, basketball was something you did until they had spring football practice. He got interest in basketball going a little bit, and we knew this because one night we came in from a road game somewhere and the students had hung him in effigy. We had lost two or three in a row, and you know what Press's comment was? He said, "We're getting to them. They're getting interested." He saw the glass as half full, and that was the truth. They were beginning to want to win some.

***

LES ROBINSON's *previous association with Press Maravich helped him break the ice in his first meeting with legendary UCLA coach John Wooden, and he also offers some insights as to why Press never again achieved the kind of success he had briefly tasted at Clemson and N.C. State:*

I was coaching Citadel in 1970–71 and our first game was against UCLA. We practiced out there the night before and the day after. Coach Wooden came back over on Saturday and visited with us. I was sitting there by myself and I told him, "Coach, I used to play and then coach for a coach who talked about you a lot and his name is Press Maravich." He said, "Oh, my goodness, what a brilliant basketball mind, but, oh, his language." I said, "Oh, I know all about that." Press was the only guy in the world who would cuss without meaning it. It was just adjectives to him that worked. Coach Wooden said one time at camp he talked to all the counselors and every day all the coaches would put a dollar in a jar to be given to Press if he could go one day without swearing, and he never got one dollar.

As for why Press never really built on the success he had achieved at N.C. State, I have an explanation why, and some people don't like it. He changed as a coach when he started coaching Pete. He didn't change as a person—he was a great person—but he became obsessed with coaching the greatest player in the game. It became more the Pistol Pete Maravich Show, and they filled every gym. He became very proud and I think that's what he wanted, but his coaching just wasn't as effective as it had been with an "ordinary" team. He did a great job at Clemson and then at N.C. State, but his LSU teams were just not the same. If there was a criticism, it is that he loved his son too much, and that's not really a criticism, it's a compliment.

If Press had stayed at N.C. State and Pete had gone somewhere else, Pete still would have been a great player and Press would have gone on to become a great coach. Pete was going to be a great player wherever, but Press wanted to coach his son. Coach (Adolph) Rupp influenced him on that. Coach Rupp had coached his son, but I remember Coach Maravich talking to some people about this. I remembered all of it, that Coach Rupp had an influence on him, a positive influence. I remember he told Coach Maravich, "Hey, if you decide not to coach him, we'll take him here at Kentucky."

❧❧❧

RALPH JUKKOLA, *another former LSU player, said he perceived that during Pete's freshman year at LSU, Press eventually lost some interest in his varsity team— which was suffering through a 3-23 season—and started spending more time watching over the freshman team:*

Press loved basketball to death and he knew basketball better than anyone I've ever known. Of course, he was very interested in what Pete did. Toward the end of our first season, I think he was more interested in what the freshmen were doing because we weren't doing much at all. Everything was basically Pete. He wanted to have winning ballclubs, but he also wanted Pete to really shine, show his stuff, and all that.

I think Press got sort of caught up in the changing times. It used to be that when you gave a kid a scholarship he went to school thinking the school owed him something, and you didn't have to worry about the off-court problems because the kids were pretty dedicated to playing. Then, starting my junior or senior year, things started changing. Press never worried too much about the matter of discipline off the court. Some of the guys ran wild, and the guys were smart enough to know that if you wanted to do something, you took Pete with you, because then Press can't do anything to you if he doesn't do it to Pete when he's with you. It's not like everyone ran around ragged, but I think it hurt Press in the long run, especially after Pete left. He was more interested in just straight basketball. All in all, Press was a good guy who would do just about anything for you if he liked you, and wouldn't do a damn thing for you if he didn't.

⋘⋙

*It didn't take **DANNY YOUNG** long as an LSU sports information student assistant to overcome Press Maravich's tough exterior to become a confidant:*

I remember going into the coaches' office the first time as an assistant in the public relations office. I had never met either Coach Maravich or Coach McCreary, but Jay immediately acknowledged me. Press was reading the paper and was holding it up high, sort of in front of his face. I was in there to get some quotes from Press for a press release or some such. Every now and then, he would lower the paper and look over at me, but he would not say a word to me. Didn't say hi, didn't say boo. I'd say something and Jay would say what he wanted Press to say. Press wouldn't acknowledge anything going on, so Jay would talk for Press.

Finally, there was something that Jay said that Press didn't agree with. The paper came down and Press cussed a blue streak, and went on and on, then he opened up. And from that point on, I don't know what it was, there had been some kind of breakthrough there with me and him, and he talked directly to me. We got to be good friends. I always felt this special feeling for Press.

One time I was in a position where I could have been drafted to go to Vietnam and Press intervened for me with the military people at LSU to get me into the ROTC program. He didn't have to do that and I never asked him to do that. I just happened to be talking when I mentioned something about the situation I was in, and he called the colonel over there and said, "Could we do this?" I ended up getting into ROTC and didn't get drafted and didn't go to Vietnam. That's just the kind of guy he was, yet he put on this big, rough exterior so no one could get real close to him.

<hr />

Another star player that Press might have had a shot at landing as a recruit his first year at LSU ended up going elsewhere in the South, and that's how Press missed out on a future NBA star with the Boston Celtics. **BUD JOHNSON** *explains how this blue-chip recruit got lost in the shuffle between the departure of Press's predecessor and Press's arrival at LSU:*

I always used to wonder what would have happened had LSU been able to get "Red" (Dave) Cowens. He ended up going to Florida State. He would have been in the same class as Pete, and they would have gone to war. A lot of people, not just us, missed on Cowens, but we had an ex-player named Dick Bailey who lived in Covington, Kentucky, and he kept after Jay McCreary to go after this kid (Cowens lived in Newport, Kentucky). He was six-six then and weighed something like 185 pounds. Well, heck, we already had guys like that—six-six, 185. We were looking for something a little bulkier.

So what happens? Florida State gets him. Press got hired in April and recruiting by then was over, So to make a long story short, Dave Cowens goes to Florida State, grows a couple of inches, and puts on some weight, and the rest is history. What a delightful fantasy that would have been. Cowens and Maravich.

⁂

*A Cowens-Maravich pairing at LSU might have been devastating for the rest of college basketball, although it's a scenario that **COWENS** never considered. But while Cowens never got to play for Press, he did get to know the chip off the old block:*

I wasn't a very good basketball player from a skills standpoint, which is why I wasn't heavily recruited at all. I had maybe twelve scholarship offers from Division I schools, and most of them were fairly local to Kentucky, other than Florida State. There was no TV and all we really had was the McDonald's Classic, so everything was pretty localized. We didn't have AAU stuff or anything like that. If you think back to that day, it was pretty unusual for Lew Alcindor to go to UCLA. Usually, West Coast guys went to West Coast schools, and same for the East Coast. I only averaged thirteen points a game my senior year in high school. And I don't recall ever hearing anything from LSU.

I did get to know Pete, though, while we were both in college. He and I were the same age, and we both worked at Lefty Driesell's basketball camp at Davidson, the summer between our junior and senior years. We had a good time at that camp. Charlie Scott and Mike Malloy were two of the other players there. I also played against Pete in the Milwaukee Classic Tournament one year. It was something like 130-100 and we set a bunch of records in that game. A whole bunch of people had a lot of rebounds and a lot of points. I also played with Pete a short time in Boston, but I remember playing against him mostly when he was with Atlanta and then New Orleans.

What I remember about him was his ability to score in a lot of different ways and that he had the total green light and that no shot was a bad shot. He shot a lot of shots from very far away from the basket, but he also had the ability to take the ball right at you and score with different shots. He was one of the best in going with both hands at you. You just never knew: He could change up on you and go left to right or right to left, and still have little hook shots, spinners, floaters, and everything else going both ways, so I always thought he was one of the better players attacking the basket.

He had a ton of confidence. One of the things I learned from him came from working with him at Lefty's camp. Lefty paid us something like forty bucks for the whole week down there sweating our buns off in June in North Carolina. Pete did an hour-long lecture on all his ballhandling tricks, and I think he made something like a hundred bucks just for that. So I watched him and took note of all the things that he did, and then I worked on all those things—the spinning the ball, throwing it up in the air and catching it different ways—all the things that he did so well during his lecture. I went home and worked on that stuff, and it helped me a lot. I did it because, what the heck, maybe I could get a hundred bucks for doing this stuff, too. That would give me something to do while working these basketball camps.

6

A PISTOL FOR
POSTERITY

Many years before he left this earth, Pete Maravich said something to the effect that he didn't want his life to be remembered for playing ten years in the NBA and then keeling over at the age of forty. Eerie, isn't it, that that's exactly what happened. A bad knee and a general discontent with his basketball career drove Maravich away from the game after ten seasons in the NBA, and then he died of a heart attack while playing a pickup game of basketball on January 5, 1988. He was forty years old.

There's so much more to Pete Maravich than his living out the uncanny prediction he had made as a young man in his twenties. He won't be remembered only for his glory days at LSU and all the things that he accomplished during a bittersweet NBA career. About five years before he died suddenly, the formerly reckless, experimental Maravich turned his life over to Jesus Christ, after which he spent many of his remaining days calmly and boldly taking the gospel and his testimony to the masses. People who had known Maravich only from his alcohol-filling yet unfulfilling days as a basketball player were stunned to see the transformed, sober Maravich in spiffy suit and tie during the eighties speaking before hundreds and even thousands of captive-audience souls, many of whom had never heard of "Pistol Pete," let alone seen him spin a basketball on his finger.

Maravich's place in history is twofold: as an incredible basketball player with seemingly supernatural ballhandling and scoring skills, and then as a modern-day Billy Sunday revealing a healed spirit and a calling for leading people to a shared eternity with Jesus Christ. Pete Maravich's impact on two divergent worlds in two different eras of his life was common in his devotion to both.

⋙⋘

*As profuse as **DICK VITALE** is with glowing adjectives when describing today's college players and coaches, there's no telling what kind of feverish-pitch level he would have hit had Pete Maravich brought his brand of Showtime basketball to today's audiences:*

He was a great playmaker. His passes, his vision, his ability on the break. It's sad that he just couldn't have played in more of a winning environment. One thing people will say is that he didn't win big, big, big, but the bottom line is that he was never surrounded with a cast. When you take great players and put them with other great people, they are able to blend, and he would have been no different. Sure, his numbers would have gone down, but it would have demonstrated his skills and ability.

In today's media environment, he would have been a soap opera superstar. He would have been on TV every night. ESPN would have loved him. I would have been down there, and I wouldn't have had enough adjectives to describe him. That's how talented he was. He was way ahead of his time. He was doing things years ago that the kids are doing now. Today you see a Kobe Bryant in the transition handling the ball and big players out on the perimeter six-six and over handling the ball—and Pistol was doing that stuff years and years ago.

Pete was a great pioneer, going between the legs and behind the back. (Bob) Cousy did it a little earlier but with a little less flair than this guy. He was a theater show, no question about it. Larry (Bird) and Magic (Johnson) were different because it wasn't just Showtime—they did the things with their inside and outside ability and blending with teams, but in each of their cases, and they would be the first ones to tell you, they had great casts around them. Magic had a guy in Kareem who was the greatest center in the low post and then other people like James Worthy. Same thing with Larry Bird with McHale and company. Pistol just didn't have that with him.

❦

Maravich helped turn basketball from a cerebral game of halfcourt X's and O's to a high-octane form of entertainment that blended Globetrotter dazzle with strategical refinement. Even today his style of basketball would be so fresh that he would still stand out as a player who brought something new to basketball. BILLY PACKER elaborates:

The game has changed so much from the time Pete left the college game and went into the pro game that he would be unbelievable in this era as a pro player. The big misnomer about Pete was that because of his scoring statistics, no one really understood how gifted he was as a ballhandler and how incredible he would have been on a great team. Unfortunately, when he entered into the NBA, the side of him that, statistically, was awesome—the scoring side— wasn't conducive to producing a winning team in the pro game. Had he in his early stages been a part of what Michael Jordan eventually had in terms of a championship-caliber team, he could have scored less, playmade more, and his pro career would have been looked upon as well as his college career. His not having won a championship works against him in the history books, particularly in an era now where people with mediocre ability who get rings are considered the equivalent of a sensational player who doesn't. Dan Marino in the NFL comes to mind as a similar example.

✦✦✦

Maravich wasn't the only LSU great who long carried the albatross of "great player never to win a championship ring," as **VITALE** *reminds us:*

Sometimes I think that's unfair. Part of it is we in the media have the mentality that unless you're Numero Uno you're an underperformer, and that's totally unfair. There have been many great people who have been in a situation—whether it be football or baseball or basketball—where they didn't have the necessary people around them. I mean, Shaq now gets a ring, and Shaq's had a great career and done a super job, but look at that Lakers team personnel-wise and it's a heck of a lot better than it's been in the past. We do an injustice to so many great talents because they don't win.

✦✦✦

Times-Picayune sportswriter **MARTY MULE** *covered Maravich as a beat writer for about half of the Pistol's pro career, and as much as Maravich and the Jazz languished in expansion-team mediocrity, Mule said it would be a big mistake to brand Maravich a loser:*

I think it's absurd to even think that. Everybody is a prisoner of their circumstances. How long did it take Michael Jordan to get a team around him so they could win a championship? Is anyone ever going to say that Charles Barkley isn't a winner because his teams never won a championship? Dan Marino? Some things you can't help. I remember the quote by (Pat) Riley (who reportedly once called Maravich "the most overrated superstar") and I always wondered what precipitated that. I always thought there was something personal about it, but I don't know. You can't always look at the surface of something and say definitively, "This is it." If you had put Pete on a great team, he would have won championships.

Scotty Robertson was the first coach of the Jazz, and now twenty-five years later—he went from the Jazz, where he was fired, to a career in the NBA as an assistant, something like four or five different teams—he has seen every team and every player in the NBA. He said a couple of years ago when you look back at Pete, he was so much better than you even remembered. Pete Maravich would be a star on any team that Scotty had seen in those twenty-five years, including Michael Jordan's championship Bulls. His level of play from twenty-five or thirty years ago would still make him a star today.

⊠⊠

Although it has been twenty years since Maravich last dribbled a basketball as an active player, former Vanderbilt player **TOM HAGEN** *says the spirit of Maravich's unique style of play lives on:*

I think he still had an impact in the pros. There are so many kids coming up who saw what he did with a basketball and realized what they would have to be capable of to be able to participate at a higher level. That's where so many offshoots of the dribbling and passing came from. He was the number-one innovator for all those moves. Bob Cousy was great, but Pete just took that and did other things that opened so many doors for other places to expand on, his being so imaginative of what he could do with a basketball. So imaginative with his spins, and turns and passes. Stuff that made people drop their mouths. The behind-the-back, forty-foot pass to a guy under the basket—so much stuff that other people hadn't even conceived of doing.

⊠⊠

TOMMY HESS, *one of Maravich's LSU teammates
and a lifelong admirer, is convinced of Maravich's
greatness in the annals of basketball history and even
quotes Shaq as a credible source backing him up in
that regard:*

Rating Pete among the all-time great basketball players is
interesting. A good way to answer that is a quote from
Shaquille O'Neal. He was asked before the Lakers played in
the championship series, "If you don't win the championship, do you still consider yourself a great player?" And
he said, "Well, if you're going to tell me that Pistol Pete"—
that's the first one he brought up—"that Pistol Pete
Maravich wasn't a great basketball player, I'm going to
punch you in the face. Has Karl Malone ever won a championship? If you're going to tell me that Karl Malone and
John Stockton aren't great players, I'm going to punch you
in the mouth." There's a lot of truth to that. Pistol Pete is
obviously one of the greatest collegiate basketball players
of all time, and if his knees hadn't gone bad on him, he
probably would have ended up with (an NBA championship) ring.

As his life changed, as Press got the cancer, and Pete did
everything he could to find ways to take care of his dad—
they had that kind of relationship—I remember I was here at
my house and my dad called me up and asked if I got a certain TV station. I turned it on and I think it was a Billy
Graham Crusade that was on. He was in a three-piece suit
and his hair was cut short, and he was giving a testimony
from his heart. He wasn't reading anything, and I was sitting
there thinking, *I cannot believe it!* The thing about that is
that we all respect our faith in our own way, but I think of
Pete back in his collegiate days and I'm reminded of South
Downs, a Baton Rouge bar that is still there. It was part of
growing up. He used to drink his long-neck Budweisers and
would shut that place down. He just loved his beer. As a
matter of fact, we were concerned about it because his

mother was an alcoholic, and as it turned out, she commit-
ted suicide. Pistol could really put that stuff away.

We were always afraid something would happen to him,
that he would get behind the wheel of that car or whatever.
And I know he must have had a tough time in Atlanta, being
the white boy who came in and signed that big contract for a
team that was predominantly black. I know one time we
went to play the University of Georgia my junior or senior
year, and Pete, by now playing with the Hawks, had set up a
meeting at some restaurant to talk with us.

I remember him sitting there and telling us that it had
been tough—not the playing-basketball part but the being-
accepted part. He had a tough time dealing with that. Pete
just wanted to have fun and play basketball, but I guess his
signing for all that money created some envy and jealousy
and stuff like that. He signed for about $2 million then,
which would be the equivalent of about $20 million now.
God rest his soul. I remember Pete telling me one time that
while basketball had given him happiness, it hadn't given
him inner strength. He tried all kinds of things—not
drugs—from yoga to hypnotism to UFO-ology. I'm just glad
his peace came through Jesus Christ.

❦

*MARAVICH, on his elusive and ultimately fruitless
search for a championship ring, a search that came to
an end in the fall of 1980 after scoring thirty-eight
points in a Celtics preseason game only to hear that
the coaching staff thought he still had a long way to go
before he could become a genuine Boston Celtic:*

All my life I had depended on the game of basketball and
considered it the constant and ultimate supplier of all my
needs. The game fed me, clothed me, brought me acceptance
into society, and paid my fare to every place I wanted to go.
A diamond ring and its significance would cap off years of
dedication to my provider. But, I started thinking how

empty I would have been if Boston had won the 1980 championship while I had been sitting on the bench. Would I have been satisfied with a ring I had not helped to win? . . . (After the thirty-eight-point game during the 1980 preseason followed by the negative hearsay from Celtic coaches) I knew the time had come to stop playing. My career was over. Dad would get no satisfaction that his son would one day be recognized as one of the world's five best. I would never play on a championship team. The third goal in the inherited dream would never become a reality. On that cold fall night in Boston I walked away from the dream. The Celtics went on that season to win the world championship.[1]

⬥⬥⬥

Being a true Christian believer and a professional athlete at the same time can be one person's tug-of-war, with the two forces often operating exclusive of each other. Maravich had rejected Christianity during his playing days while he played with fire, yet he accepted Christ after his retirement and lived out his life as a disciple of Christ as enthused about taking his testimony and Scripture to unbelievers as he had been taking the rock to the hole a decade earlier. **TOM HAGEN,** *a born-again Christian and former Vanderbilt player who went head to head with Maravich in college, admires the Pistol more for his profession of faith than his profession of basketball:*

The environment that you're in as a big-time athlete puts you into a world where so many people around you aren't Christians. It's so easy to compromise. It's hard to share your Christianity when so many other guys around you are talking about women or what not. You're acting like you agree with them not because you want to, but because you want to be liked. It's that self-esteem thing. Even though you're making all that money and you're the stud, you want everybody to like you. Unless you have that strong foundation, when you face all these worldly temptations and confrontations, it's almost easier to back away and go with the flow. To see younger people that maintain these ideals is what's so rewarding for me to see—young people who have the discipline to maintain their faith. That's what being a real Christian is about.

⚛

BOB SANDFORD, *who befriended Maravich when they were high school teenagers in Raleigh, maintained for moving into it. Josh suffered severe head injuries that, to the astonishment of attending physicians, almost completely healed within several days while the Pistol lay next to his son in a hospital bed, praying throughout the day and night:*

Pete talked to me a lot about his Christianity. His son falling through the shaft in the house was the thing that woke him up. You've got to remember, Pete was the kind of guy who could do nothing in moderation. That was his biggest downfall. As far as basketball, he was obsessed with it. Then we'd go out to a party and we'd drink two or three beers, and he would drink ten. And then he got into karate. I remember when he went to Atlanta, I went to spend a week with him in the summertime, and when I woke up in the morning he wouldn't even be there. He'd been down at the gym a block or two away, and I'd walk down there and he'd be there in the gym from like nine in the morning until nine o'clock at night, and he earned a black belt in like a year's time.

From karate, he went into yoga, and then he got into being a vegetarian and that about drove me crazy. He'd come to my house, where he wouldn't eat anything, only pick up every jar and read the labels. He wouldn't eat this, that, or the other. Finally, when all this stuff happened with his son, he told me, "You're not going to believe this, but God spoke to me. He woke me up in bed. I woke up Jackie and she thought I was crazy." He said the Lord spoke to him.

Pete and Jaeson, the older of his two sons, yuk it up along with Maravich's longtime pal Bob Sandford. This was in June 1980, not long before Pete would retire after rejoining the Celtics for training camp that fall.

Being the type of person he was in doing nothing in moderation, he started going around witnessing and even came back to Broughton High School in Raleigh and witnessed for the student body. He was doing tremendous things for young people all over everywhere. When he was in high school, the only thing that was on his mind was being the best basketball player that he could be. He didn't make good grades in high school, but he was a very sharp guy and if you ever listened to any of his testimonies and the way he could speak to a crowd, he could quote Scriptures from the Bible left and right. He was very intelligent. He just picked it up so easy. It's almost like he was given some power to where he could just absorb it. Verses came off the tip of his tongue in any situation that came up. He was unbelievable in that aspect.

∞

During his "salad days" as a vegetarian, Maravich would occasionally try to sneak in a beloved steak every now and then, although he got caught at least once when LSU acquaintances **DONALD RAY KENNARD** *and Bud Johnson happened to stumble across Pete eating alone in a corner of a restaurant, as Kennard recalls with a chuckle:*

He had just been inducted into the Louisiana Sports Hall of Fame in Nacogdoches, Louisiana. Bud and I got there early on Friday, probably like six o'clock, pulled into a Holiday Inn, went to our room and put our clothes up, and then we walked down to the restaurant. I look into the far corner of the restaurant, and there's Pete Maravich sitting back there. He looks around and sees us coming, and he's got a plate full of food. He takes his napkin off of his lap and covers his food. I said, "Pete, what are you doing?" And he said, "Well, I figured you would catch me doing something I hadn't done in several years." I said, "What's that?" And he said, "You know, I became a vegetarian and I haven't had a steak in three to five years. I'm up here where nobody would know me in this little town, and I just wanted to see what a steak tasted like. And now you walk in and catch me violating my personal code of no more meat. So it means I'm not supposed to eat this steak, so I'm not going to eat it." So he shoved back in his chair and talked with us but didn't eat the steak. I'm not lying: You can't make this stuff up.

∞

The last time **BILL TROTT** *saw his former high school teammate was when Maravich returned to Broughton*

in late 1987 to have his jersey retired at Broughton
High School. It was a memorable meeting between old
friends, mostly because Maravich was dead about a
week later:

We talked for about four hours that afternoon they retired
his jersey. He was talking about different subjects. One was
about how tough life was in the NBA, and basically he said
that where most people in that generation of the NBA were
taking drugs, he never took bad drugs. But he did become an
alcoholic. He told me how every night after the game, they
had coolers of beers in the locker room and then someone
would take them on the bus—they were just ushered out of
the arena—to the bus and then to the airplane, and the
whole time they were just drinking beer and would wake up
the next morning and not remember what city he was in. He
would then sleep until about four o'clock in the afternoon
and then get up and start pumping himself up for the game
that night, and then start over the next day.

He loved his children and he talked about how much he
enjoyed playing basketball with them. The other thing I
remember distinctly about talking to him that time was his
talking about his father's cancer and his mother's suicide,
and how now he had achieved peace with his life and God.
His father had had a really debilitating type of cancer for the
last year or so and had gone to live at home. He had shrunk
down to something like 125 pounds. Pete would have to
carry him from one room to another and give him his shots
of painkiller, and all that. Through the whole process, it was
an actual religious experience for Pete to do that with his
father, and they settled out any old problems they had had
growing up.

One of the things Pete said was that during the course of
looking after his father, he had hurt his shoulder and it took
about a year to get over his shoulder problem. That's why he
hadn't been able to play any basketball or get any exercise for
about a year, and he had lost his extremely good conditioning.

Pete had always been in such good shape, that even annual medical examinations couldn't detect his congenital heart condition that ultimately killed him. I think what happened is that he got out of shape while helping his father and developed the shoulder problem, and after getting over the shoulder problem he tried to go out and play basketball in California. But when he started playing, his conditioning was such that his heart couldn't overcome it. It was kind of tragic how he died playing basketball. Yet it was sort of fitting, too. One of the last things he said to me was, "I could die tomorrow and be happy. If I didn't get to live this life any longer, I would be happy and at peace with this world." And then a week later he died.

⚬⚬

DAVE KRIDER, *the veteran national high school sports reporter, considers Maravich one of the greatest players he ever saw, although it was Maravich's Christianity that meant the most to him:*

The best thing about Pete Maravich to me concerns the fact that my wife, Lois, and I sponsor the Fellowship of Christian Athletes in LaPorte. Late in his life, after he retired and became a Christian, he was going to speak at nearby Bethel College, and I had a bunch of my kids all fired up to go over there and hear him speak. But what happened was that Pete had his heart attack and died before he could get to speak there. We were so crushed by that, because we wanted to meet him personally and tell him how happy we were for him. I have heard some tapes of the witnesses he gave after that, and, I'll tell you what, he gave some really terrific testimonies.

⚬⚬

*Former Tennessee player **BILL JUSTUS**, one of the Vols players who had chased Maravich around a basketball court, caught up with Maravich in the eighties when the*

*Pistol was giving his testimony before a church full of
youngsters in Houston:*

I just remember how real sincere he was. I had had no clue
as to some of the things he had gone through while at LSU
and how he had continued to fight through some demons
while he was in pro ball. Then he changed his life and
became a better person, somebody who believed he needed
to give something back, and he had a good message.

The day he died, I was playing tennis at an indoor club,
and someone came in on the court and told me. It was
amazing the impact it had on me. I slumped down even
though I hadn't seen him in such a long time and hadn't
competed against him since college, and I thought what a
bad loss that was. A terrible thing for his family and everyone else, too. He was one of those guys with a creative
genius that you lose too soon, and it seems like that happens a lot. Maybe you just can't see Pete getting old. It's
astonishing that he didn't have some kind of medical sign
before this. This was something he had carried with him his
whole life.

❧❧❧

HAGEN *remembers where he was and what he was
doing when he heard that Maravich had died young—
he was getting ready to take his YMCA team through a
basketball practice:*

I remember going to coach a YMCA ballclub that evening.
They were eight or nine years old and probably didn't know
who Pete Maravich was. I explained to them that we had lost
one of the great basketball players of our time and to go
home and talk to their dads about who he was. Hearing
about his death was one of those feelings where your heart
goes down to your feet. It really took a lot from me. Pete
went into his Christianity so wholeheartedly and just didn't
stay out on the fringes. He went in there full-scale, talking to

the younger generation. He was determined to make a big difference. You wonder why people die young and you wonder why the Lord took him home early when it looks like he could have been such a strong testimony for a long time. But he touched a lot of lives.

※※※

Twelve years after Maravich's death, SANDFORD still often gazes at the eight-by-ten-inch framed photo of Maravich he has on his office wall, remembering back to the last time he saw Maravich—the week Maravich came back to Raleigh to have his high school basketball jersey retired:

I picked him up at the airport that Thursday, and he stayed with me Thursday and Friday night. They retired his jersey on Friday night and dedicated the tournament to him. I then put him on a plane Saturday morning. He went back to Louisiana and I think he left the following Thursday to go out to California. We had talked about everything those two days he was here. He had had a few health problems, but nothing with his heart. He had had a thing with palsy affecting the muscles in his face some. But he was getting over it. Had no idea there was anything with his heart. He was a very, very dear friend. His wife, Jackie, too, and his sons are good boys. I think about them every day.

※※※

DR. JAMES DOBSON, who has become one of the world's best-known proponents of applying scriptural truth to family life and a leading critic of political correctness as president of Focus on the Family, was one of those playing pickup basketball with the Pistol in California on January 5, 1988, when Maravich collapsed during a water break after about forty-five minutes of playing four-on-four, with one of the other players being another ex-NBAer, Ralph Drollinger. In

essence, Maravich died in Dobson's arms, as Dobson
recalls in his book Life on the Edge:

I hurried over to where Pete lay and still expected him to get up laughing. But then I saw that he was having a seizure. I held his tongue to keep his air passage open and called for the other guys to come help me. The seizure lasted about twenty seconds, and then Pete stopped breathing. We started CPR immediately but were never able to get another heartbeat or another breath. Pistol Pete Maravich, one of the world's greatest athletes, died there in my arms at forty years of age. . . . How he was able to do such incredible exploits on the basketball court for so many years is a medical mystery. He was destined to drop dead at a fairly young age, and only God knows why it happened during the brief moment when his path crossed mine.[2]

Maravich was in California at the time planning to join
Dr. Dobson to tape an interview for Dobson's radio
program, but the interview never took place. Still,
Maravich had already spent several years proclaiming
his Christianity and taking his message to audiences
around the country, as **DOBSON** *remembers:*

Five years before he died he came to a personal knowledge, a personal relationship with Jesus Christ after a very troubled and rebellious life. He went from a man who was lost and without meaning, without purpose, to a person who was filled to overflowing with a love of the Lord. When he died there on that gymnasium floor, he had a T-shirt on that said, "Looking unto Jesus." You just engage him in a conversation for just a few minutes and you find yourself talking about what the Lord had done for him. That was the legacy that he left.[3]

Maravich was close to indiscriminate in giving his Christian testimony to listeners, and one of those who heard the good word from Maravich was **MULE**, *who remembers the occasion as a meeting between the two during the time Maravich was being inducted into the Louisiana Sports Hall of Fame. Mule was supposed to be interviewing Maravich for a story, but the tables were turned for the better part of that two-hour session:*

I hadn't seen him in a while, and I was going to do a story on him. We went and sat by the pool. It ended up being very little of my interviewing him, and it was more his passing along the gospel to me. Finally after about two hours I had to break it off, saying, "Pete, I've got to go write this story." He was just getting wound up with this thing.

Every year before the ceremony, they always have film clips of the people who are getting inducted and have gone in before, and they're always nice to watch. But I swear to God, when you see the clips on Pete, it wakes you up. It startles you with what you see on film. You almost forget what you had seen in real life. You're kind of dozing along while the film is playing and all of a sudden it's like a shot of adrenaline hits you when you're watching some of these passes and plays. Even if he were playing today with the stuff he was doing then, it would still have the feel of being fresh and innovative. The Jazz had a reunion in New Orleans two or three years ago and I did a series on the old Jazz. I remember talking to Butch van Breda Kolff, and he said, "Today in the NBA they're playing the game Pete brought to it. The things that he was criticized for, a lot, while he was a player are everyday plays now. They may not do it as well as Pete, but they're all doing it."

Pete Maravich to basketball is like what Elvis Presley was to music: His influence can't be measured, and a lot of people don't give him the credit he deserves.

MARAVICH probably didn't have a death wish, although there are indications that he had at least accepted the inevitability of it:

He sounded prepared for death and, in the eulogy of his father, Press, eight months before his own death, appeared to know it was about to come. Maravich talked of sitting beside the bed of his father in the waning moments of his long bout with bone cancer and whispering in his ear, "I want you to know, Dad, that I will be with you soon." If there was a consistent, tragic theme for Maravich it was in the timing of things: accolades that came a little too late, a style of play that was ahead of its era, a life that ended all too soon.[4]

⸎

MARAVICH, on his experience during the night in which he turned his life over to Jesus Christ:

I cried out to God, saying, "I've cursed you and I've spit on you. I've mocked you and used your name in vain. . . . Oh, God, can you forgive me, can you forgive me? Please, save me, please." . . . I remembered the late sixties and the day in California when I rejected the idea of a personal relationship with Jesus Christ because of what it might do to interfere with my career goals. Now, sixteen years later, I wondered if God had forsaken me because of all the things I had done or not done. . . . Suddenly without warning, I heard a voice say, "be strong. Lift thine own heart." The voice seemed to reverberate throughout the room. . . . It was an audible voice! . . . I prayed a simple prayer as best I could. "Jesus Christ, come into my life . . . forgive me of my sin. I believe with all my heart that you died for me and rose from the grave so I would have eternal life. Make me the person you want me to be." Through this simple act of surrender, the void that once loomed so large was filled.[5]

⸎

*To listen to **DONALD RAY KENNARD** talk about some circumstances surrounding Maravich's death is to be reminded that there must be a God and that "coincidences" might actually be events directed by divine intervention:*

As of Christmas in 1987 I still hadn't read Pete's own book, which had been published earlier that year. He had given me an autographed copy that I had placed on our Christmas tree. So the night of the day he died, I get home, probably around 7:30, and I decided to pick up the book and take a look. Right off the bat I see where he had signed it with a reference to John 14:6. Well, everyone knows what John 3:16 is, but I didn't know John 14:6 from John 14:27. So I opened my Bible and had just found the words when the phone rang. It was some lady looking for my wife. And I said, "Ma'am, she's in Lake Charles." She happened to ask me what I was doing, and I said, "You know, Pete Maravich died today and he left me an autographed copy of his book and it included a couple verses of Scripture for me to read. And right now, I'm reading John 14:6." And she said, "Let's read it together. I'm reading the same verse." Now get this: She's reading the same verse in her Bible that I had just turned to, and she said let's read it in unison. I thought to myself, I'm going to take my bath and go to bed.

Let me tell you what happened that morning, on January 5. That day we, the state legislature, had had a Highway Transportation Committee hearing in New Orleans. I went down on the fourth of January because I had to chair that committee. I stayed overnight at an old historic hotel. It was really cold the next morning, overcast and with a misting rain. I was leaving the hotel when I decided to check out a men's store right next to the hotel. I was looking through the window of the store when I happened to notice that there was one other person on that same street, probably a block and a half away and walking toward me. My first thought was, *Hey, there's another guy like me out in this cold weather.*

And then I noticed he had a little gunnysack over his shoulder. As he got closer to me, I could see that he had on sunglasses. He got right up to me and then said, "Aren't you Donald Ray Kennard?" And I said, "Yeah." And he said, "I'm Ronnie Maravich." I said, "Ronnie, I have not seen you in six or seven years. Where in the world have you been?" And he said, "I'm still doing the same thing, working in New Orleans, bartending." Then he said, "I was just going to wash my clothes."

Now, think of this—Pete is in Los Angeles, California, with James Dobson, and this is like nine o'clock in the morning our time, which is seven o'clock in California. And I said, "Well, Ronnie, how is Pete doing?" And he said, "Donald, you know, since Dad died, Pete and I have developed the best relationship that we've had in our lives. We spent Thanksgiving together, we spent Christmas together, and I'm going to tell you what, they're fixing to start filming the story of his life at Southeastern Louisiana. Pete has turned everything over to me. He's going to let me be his manager. Why don't you come over to Hammond in about two weeks and watch us film the movie because you know Pete will be around on the set." And I said, "Ronnie, you just don't know how good it is to see you." And he said, "Isn't this ironic how we bumped into each other, the only two people on the street when it's cold and nasty?" And I said, "I hope to see you in the near future."

So I go on to my Highway Committee hearing. Then I get back into my car and I'm riding down the interstate highway back to Baton Rouge, and I hear on the radio, "Bulletin, bulletin, bulletin. Pete Maravich passed away this morning in a pickup basketball game." Then I get home and have the thing with the lady on the phone. Then in the middle of the night, I'm sound asleep when I get a call from Dale Brown. He's a person who stays up all night long. I had the academic program at LSU for twenty-five years, and I had been the first guy he met when he came to LSU. After all, you've got to keep your ballplayers academically sound.

So he said, "Donald Ray, this is Dale. What are you doing?" And I said, "What do you think I'm doing? I'm sleeping." And he said, "Look, man, we've got to do something for Pete." Keep in mind, Pete had been kind of estranged from LSU for eight or ten years. And he said, "What do you want to do for him?" And I said, "Well, Dale, let's think about this for a while." He said, "What would you suggest?" And I said, "We could do a bust of him, put it right out in front of the Assembly Center." And he said, "Why don't we rename the street between the Assembly Center and the football stadium Pete Maravich Boulevard." I said, "Dale, with the football stadium on the right and the Assembly Center on the left, I don't know how that would mesh, you know what I mean, with basketball and football. I don't know how people would accept that because Tiger Stadium has been there since the thirties and the Maravich Center hasn't been there very long." So we kept talking and I said, "Why don't we name it the Pete Maravich Assembly Center." And he said, "That ain't a bad idea. Would you look at introducing the bill?" So I coauthored the bill with Francis Thompson in 1988. It passed the House 102-0, and then the Senate, 23-10.

We didn't have the wake until Thursday night. I decided to get there early with all the athletes coming in because I knew all of them and wanted to have a chance to speak to them. I pull up in the parking lot and there was not one car there yet. The wake was supposed to start at six, and this was about 5:20. I pull up in the parking lot and park perpendicular to the curb. Suddenly, here comes this guy in a gold Chrysler and he swerved in there, pulling right up beside me and gets out. Guess who that was? Ronnie Maravich. He gets out of the car, runs over, hugs me, and starts crying. He said, "Donnie Ray, little did we know when we were talking on Monday or Tuesday (don't remember—it was January 5) Pete was dying. Is this unbelievable?" I said, "Ronnie, this is unbelievable. You and I were the first ones here and you park right beside me in the parking lot before I even know that's you."

I got tears in my eyes. He said, "I'm so glad that we talked." And I told him, "Ronnie, you know the last time I saw Pete was when they had him come to LSU in November at the Assembly Center. I looked up there where he was sitting in the stands and there was just a throng of people there. Pete had sent me a note to go see him. I went up there and he said he just wanted to visit with me. He was there with Jackie and the kids. I said, "Pete, great to see you. You look good, you look great, and it looks like you're enjoying retirement. I'm going to go and let you have your time with people here who really want to greet you and be with you." So I went back down to my seat, and that was the last time I saw him.

⌘

PETE MARAVICH's prayer at the 1987 NBA All-Star Chapel:

Heavenly Father, we have gathered here this morning before thy presence with thanksgiving and praise. We sing in our hearts for joy to you, O Lord, and we know that you shout joyfully because you are the rock of our salvation. Father, your word says that "man is like a mere breath; his days like a passing shadow." Make us realize the shortness of our days here upon this earth, so that we will begin to utilize the precious time you give to each of us for the winning of souls to the kingdom. Give to us that know you the desire and power to boldly and confidently witness what Christ has done in each of our lives.

Your word also says in Matthew 16:26, "For what will a man be profited if he gains the whole world, and forfeits his soul; or what will a man give in exchange for his soul?" What upon this earth is worth the eternal loss of one's soul? Father, there is no amount of money that one can have, or material things that one can possess, nor prestigious awards one can receive, or even power that one can own which will ever fill the void and Godly shaped vacuum that is present within the hearts of all people who have said no to the Savior. For all that is external and physical is but for a fleeting, temporary moment, compared to the inexplicable joy when the truth of Jesus Christ comes home into one's heart, and a lasting peace which is permanent and eternal.

My prayer this morning, Father, is for the light of the gospel of Christ to penetrate the darkness here this weekend; the deceived and even the stupid for your word says in Psalms 149:10, "The senseless and stupid shall perish alike." I also pray for an injury-free game and travel mercies to all as they leave for home. I pray for all these things in the magnificent, wonderful, name of Jesus, Amen.[6]

PETE MARAVICH'S CAREER STATISTICS

LSU—GAME BY GAME

Freshman Year, 1966–67

Game Result	FG-FGA	FT-FTA	Pts.	Rebs.	Assts.
LSU 119, Southeastern 70	19-41	12-15	50	14	11
LSU 83, Baton Rouge Hawks 79	9-31	16-20	34	22	8
LSU 74, Loyola 72	13-32	8-12	34	8	3
LSU 96, Tulane 78	15-38	6-10	36	12	9
LSU 113, Mississippi State 80	13-30	9-10	35	9	9
LSU 97, Ole Miss 76	15-31	13-16	43	8	4
LSU 88, Auburn 73	17-28	10-12	44	6	5
LSU 98, Bordens 68	17-30	6-9	40	11	18
LSU 97, Southern Mississippi 82	(Did not play)				
LSU 69, Tulane 68 (OT)	13-39	5-7	31	8	6
LSU 111, Baton Rouge Hawks 84	26-51	14-16	66	9	9
LSU 105, Loyola 59	20-36	10-10	50	14	4
LSU 136, Saint Mark's 89	15-38	20-21	50	11	7
LSU 108, Auburn 71	21-41	15-18	57	7	4
LSU 94, Southern Mississippi 86	15-29	12-12	42	11	4
LSU 106, Mississippi State 71	19-32	15-17	53	5	8
LSU 110, Ole Miss 98	14-41	17-21	45	15	9
Tennessee 75, LSU 74	12-36	7-9	31	6	6

Season Totals:

FG-FGA: 273-604 (.452)
FT-FTA: 195-234 (.833)
Points: 741

Scoring avg.: 43.6
Rebounds avg.: 10.4
Assists avg.: 6.9

Sophomore Year, 1967–68

Game Result	FG-FGA	FT-FTA	Pts.	Rebs.	Assts.
LSU 97, Tampa 81	20-50	8-9	48	16	4
LSU 87, Texas 74	15-34	12-16	42	5	5
LSU 90, Loyola 56	22-43	7-11	51	9	4
Wisconsin 96, LSU 94	16-40	10-13	42	9	6
Florida State 130, LSU 100	17-41	8-10	42	5	9
LSU 81, Ole Miss 68	17-34	12-13	46	11	3
LSU 111, Mississippi State 87	22-40	14-16	58	8	3
LSU 81, Alabama 70	10-30	10-11	30	6	5
LSU 76, Auburn 72	20-38	15-17	55	9	1
Florida 97, LSU 90	9-22	14-17	32	10	8
LSU 79, Georgia 76	14-37	14-17	42	11	5
LSU 100, Tulane 91	20-42	12-15	52	5	8
LSU 104, Clemson 81	14-29	5-6	33	6	2
Kentucky 121, LSU 95	19-51	14-17	52	11	2
Vanderbilt 99, LSU 91	22-57	10-15	54	6	3
Kentucky 109, LSU 96	16-38	12-15	44	8	3
Tennessee 87, LSU 67	9-34	3-3	21	6	0
Auburn 74, LSU 69	18-47	13-13	49	6	1
LSU 93, Florida 92 (OT)	17-48	13-15	47	7	3
Georgia 78, LSU 73	20-47	11-18	51	4	2
LSU 99, Alabama 89	24-52	11-13	59	12	3
LSU 94, Mississippi State 83	13-38	8-12	34	7	7
LSU 99, Tulane 92	21-47	13-15	55	5	0
Ole Miss 87, LSU 85	13-26	14-16	40	4	8
Tennessee 74, LSU 71	7-18	3-4	17	3	1
Vanderbilt 115, LSU 86	17-39	8-11	42	6	9

Season Totals:

FG-FGA:	432-1,022 (.422)	Scoring avg.:	43.8
FT-FTA:	274-338 (.810)	Rebounds avg.:	7.5
Points:	1,138	Assists avg.:	4.0

Junior Year, 1968–69

Game Result	FG-FGA	FT-FTA	Pts.	Rebs.	Assts.
LSU 109, Loyola 82	22-34	8-9	52	7	11
LSU 86, Clemson 85	10-32	18-22	38	4	4
Tulane 101, LSU 99 (2-OT)	20-48	15-20	55	7	2
LSU 93, Florida 89 (OT)	17-32	11-15	45	8	5
LSU 98, Georgia 89	18-33	11-16	47	10	5
LSU 84, Wyoming 78	14-34	17-24	45	6	2
LSU 101, Oklahoma City 85	19-36	2-5	40	8	7
LSU 94, Duquesne 91	18-36	17-21	53	2	6
Alabama 85, LSU 82	19-49	4-4	42	10	5
Vanderbilt 94, LSU 92	15-30	8-13	38	4	3
Auburn 90, LSU 71	16-41	14-18	46	5	5
Kentucky 108, LSU 96	20-48	12-14	52	11	2
Tennessee 81, LSU 68	8-18	5-8	21	4	2
LSU 120, Pittsburgh 79	13-34	14-18	40	8	11
Ole Miss 84, LSU 81 (OT)	11-33	9-13	31	11	5
LSU 95, Mississippi State 71	14-32	5-6	33	11	10
LSU 81, Alabama 75	15-30	8-12	38	5	6
Tulane 110, LSU 94	25-51	16-20	66	10	1
Florida 95, LSU 79	14-41	22-27	50	6	2
LSU 93, Auburn 81	20-44	14-15	54	3	5
Vanderbilt 85, LSU 83	14-33	7-8	35	8	8
Kentucky 103, LSU 89	21-53	3-7	45	5	2
Tennessee 87, LSU 63	8-18	4-8	20	3	7
Ole Miss 78, LSU 76	21-39	7-11	49	3	1
LSU 99, Mississippi State 89	20-49	15-19	55	4	5
LSU 90, Georgia 80 (2-OT)	21-48	16-25	58	6	4

Season Totals:

FG-FGA	433-976 (.444)	Scoring avg.:	44.2
FT-FTA:	282-378 (.746)	Rebounds avg.:	6.5
Points:	1,148	Assists avg.:	4.9

Senior Year, 1969–70

Game Result	FG-FGA	FT-FTA	Pts.	Rebs.	Assts.
LSU 94, Oregon State 72	14-32	15-19	43	5	7
LSU 100, Loyola 87	18-36	9-10	45	6	6
LSU 109, Vanderbilt 86	26-54	9-10	61	10	5
LSU 97, Tulane 91	17-42	12-19	46	4	5
Southern Cal 101, LSU 98	18-43	14-16	50	6	4
LSU 111, Clemson 103	22-30	5-8	49	6	9
LSU 76, Oregon State 68	8-23	30-31	46	1	8
UCLA 133, LSU 84	14-42	10-12	38	4	7
LSU 80, St. John's 70	20-44	13-16	53	8	1
Yale 97, LSU 94	13-28	8-11	34	5	8
LSU 90, Alabama 83	22-42	11-18	55	7	2
Auburn 79, LSU 70	18-46	8-11	44	6	2
Kentucky 109, LSU 96	21-44	13-15	55	5	4
LSU 71, Tennessee 59	12-23	5-7	29	4	9
LSU 109, Ole Miss 86	21-46	11-15	53	5	12
LSU 109, Mississippi State 91	21-40	7-9	49	3	6
LSU 97, Florida 75	20-38	12-16	52	9	7
Alabama 106, LSU 104	26-57	17-21	69	5	4
LSU 127, Tulane 114	18-45	13-15	49	4	6
LSU 94, Florida 85	16-35	6-10	38	6	8
LSU 99, Vanderbilt 89	14-46	10-13	38	5	3
LSU 70, Auburn 64	18-46	10-15	46	8	4
LSU 88, Georgia 86	17-34	3-6	37	2	6
Kentucky 121, LSU 105	23-42	18-22	64	4	7
Tennessee 88, LSU 87	10-24	10-13	30	7	6
LSU 103, Ole Miss 90	13-43	9-14	35	9	4
LSU 97, Mississippi State 87	22-44	11-13	55	2	8
LSU 99, Georgia 88	16-37	9-10	41	3	11
(NIT) LSU 83, Georgetown 82			20		
(NIT) LSU 97, Oklahoma 94			37		
(NIT) Marquette 101, LSU 79			20		
(NIT) Army 75, LSU 68		(Did not play)			

Season Totals:

FG-FGA:	522-1,168 (.447)	Scoring avg.:	44.5
FT-FTA:	337-436 (.773)	Rebounds avg.:	5.3
Points:	1,381	Assists avg.:	6.2

LSU CAREER TOTALS (varsity only):

FG-FGA:	1,387-3,166 (.438)	Scoring avg.:	44.2
FT-FTA:	893-1,152 (.775)	Rebounds avg.:	6.4
Points:	3,667	Assists avg.:	5.1

NBA—SEASON BY SEASON

Season	1970–71	1971–72	1972–73	1973–74
Team	Atlanta	Atlanta	Atlanta	Atlanta
G	81	66	79	76
FG%	.458	.427	.441	.457
FT%	.800	.811	.800	.826
Points	1,880	1,275	2,063	2,107
Average	23.2	19.3	26.1	27.7
Reb. Avg.	3.7	3.9	4.4	4.9
Assts. Avg.	4.4	6.0	6.9	5.2

Season	1974–75	1975–76	1976–77	1977–78
Team	New Orleans	New Orleans	New Orleans	New Orleans
G	79	62	73	50
FG%	.419	.459	.433	.444
FT%	.811	.811	.835	.870
Points	1,700	1,604	2,273	1,352
Average	21.5	25.9	31.1	27.0
Reb. Avg.	5.3	4.8	5.1	3.6
Assts. Avg.	6.2	5.4	5.4	6.7

Season	1978–79	1979–80	NBA Career Totals
Team	New Orleans	Utah/Boston	
G	49	43	658
FG%	.421	.449	.441
FT%	.841	.867	.820
Points	1,105	589	15,948
Average	22.6	13.7	24.2
Reb. Avg.	2.5	1.8	4.2
Assts. Avg.	5.0	1.9	5.4

NOTES

Chapter 1: THE CAROLINA KID

1. Maravich, Pete, and Darrel Campbell, *Pistol Pete: Heir to a Dream* (Nashville: Thomas Nelson, 1987), p. 57.
2. Ibid., p. 74.
3. Ibid., p. 71.
4. Ibid., p. 92.
5. Ibid., pp. 93-94.

Chapter 2: TIGER TOWN

1. Maravich and Campbell, p. 101.
2. Ibid., pp. 103-4.
3. Ibid., pp. 105-6.
4. Kirkpatrick, Curry, "The Coed Boppers' Top Cat," *Sports Illustrated*, originally published in 1968 and reprinted November 28, 1994.

Chapter 3: THE PROS, AND POETRY IN MOTION

1. Maravich and Campbell, p. 150.
2. Ibid., p. 145.
3. Ibid., p. 162.
4. Ibid., p. 166.

Chapter 4: SHOWTIME

1. Maravich and Campbell, p. 109.
2. Barnes, Craig, "Pistol Pete Typical of Age," *Charlotte News and Observer*, December 23, 1969.
3. Kirkpatrick, Curry, "A Singular Showman," *Sports Illustrated*, January 18, 1988.

4. Goldaper, Sam, "The Maravich Show Moves in Friday," *New York Times*, March 1970 (exact date unknown).

5. Fowler, Scott, *Charlotte Observer*, April 3, 1994.

6. Goldaper.

7. Coulbourn, Keith, "Close-Up of a Baby Hawk: Is Basketball Evolving Toward Something Fascinatingly New with the Arrival of Pistol Pete?" *Atlanta Journal and Constitution Magazine*, November 22, 1970.

8. Ibid.

9. Barnes, "Pistol Pete Typical of Age."

10. Ibid.

CHAPTER 5: FULLCOURT PRESS

1. Maravich and Campbell, p. 67.

CHAPTER 6: A PISTOL FOR POSTERITY

1. Maravich and Campbell, pp. 184, 186.

2. Dobson, James, *Life on the Edge: A Young Adult's Guide to a Meaningful Future* (Dallas: Word, 1995), pp. 269-70.

3. Dobson, James, and Mike Trott, "A Tribute to Pete Maravich," audiotape (Colorado Springs: Focus on the Family), copyright 1988, 1993.

4. Adande, J. A., *Los Angeles Times*, January 1998 (exact date unknown).

5. Maravich and Campbell, pp. 192, 193.

6. Maravich, Pete, reprinted in "Order of Service" pamphlet for Maravich's January 1988 funeral service.

INDEX